# A
# FRACTURED
# LIFE

*A Memoir*

☾

*This is me with a cousin and my mother. (It's the only picture that I have with my mother).*

# A
# FRACTURED
# LIFE

*A Memoir*

## Shabnam Samuel

GREEN PLACE BOOKS | *Brattleboro, Vermont*

GREEN WRITERS PRESS is a Vermont-based publisher whose mission is to
spread a message of hope and renewal through the words and images we publish.
Throughout we will adhere to our commitment to preserving and protecting the
natural resources of the earth. To that end, a percentage of our proceeds will be
donated to environmental activist groups and the author's charity of choice, No
Hungry Child (nohungrychild.in). Green Writers Press gratefully acknowledges
support from individual donors, friends, and readers to help support the
environment and our publishing initiative. GREEN PLACE BOOKS curates books
that tell literary and compelling stories with a focus on writing about place.

GREEN
PLACE
BOOKS

GReen
writers
press

*Giving Voice to Writers & Artists Who Will Make the World a Better Place*

Green Writers Press | Brattleboro, Vermont
www.greenwriterspress.com

ISBN: 978-1-7320815-9-8

COVER DESIGN: Filomena Thompson
COVER PHOTO OF THE AUTHOR FROM HER COLLECTION.

# Contents

❨ ❩

*For my son, Ankoor.*


*For never giving up on me through all the turbulence.*

*For showing me what unconditional love means.*

*This book is for you.*


☾

*I am beginning to realize, that it was not always the fault
in my stars. There were other faulty stars before me that
dimmed my light.*

# Introduction

❰ ❱

WHEN I DECIDED TO WRITE MY STORY, I did it
to prove that I exist.

The title of my book, *A Fractured Life*, came to
me while I sat one day to examine every decade of my life for
the last five decades. Every decade that I paused and reflected
on, there seemed to be a split, a splint, a tear, a rupture, and a
fracture. Every decade was connected. Every year in chrono-
logical order that led to a decade had heartbreak, confusion,
darkness, questions, and most times, dark, murky secrets that
were either mine or passed down from a generation or two.
I had, and still have, no idea how to deal with the dark that
seems to follow me around like a faithful companion.

I have still not found the answers I have been searching
for all my life. Sometimes new experiences or new encoun-
ters lead to clarifications, but I still seem to be unable to find

the answers that I looked for even as a child, gazing up at the stars and the moon and wondering if I would ever twinkle or shine.

All my life, I have been a lost soul, a lost person, a person who seemed to have been retrieved from a lost and found department. Never was I claimed by a unit or a nuclear family. Never was I told, you look like your father, or you sound just like your mother. Never was I tagged: Here, you belong to us.

Yet, yet I have found my voice, maybe a few decades late, but here I am, trying to tell people that even though everything in your life seems ruptured, fractured, or hopeless, you can still find your way through the pain, through the tears, and through the little things that bring you joy.

And it is never too late. Never too late to lay the cupboard of your family skeletons bare. Never too late to tell people you belong. Never too late to do away with a part of your culture that silences you, that has ingrained in you that loyalty, secrets, and the bad stuff all stay inside the family compound wall.

The second reason I write this book is to tell women, children, men, cousins, sisters, and brothers to always be true to yourself, to speak your voice and don't let the unpleasant memories crush your soul.

### Life

What happens between the awakenings of my soul
And the harsh realities of stories untold?
I hopscotch through the stones

Hopping
To skip the ones that burn
But imprinted in my mind
Is sadness of every kind
Get up I say
Bury the pain away
Life can be wonderful in different ways.

Every time that I have fallen, I have tried to stand up again. Every time that I have been down under water, I have tried to swim up again. Sometimes on shaky legs, and sometimes on uneven ground, and a lot of times on quicksand, but always drawing from a strength that allows me to stand upright, but never lets me walk away from me. This strength has kept me alive, has kept me lonely, has kept me sad, has kept me happy, and it is this strength that allows me to write, even though I have lived almost all my life in shadows.

This is my story. I write to prove that I exist.

# PART I

（ ）

PART 1

# 1
# *My Grandmother*

❨ ❩

*Sitting on the coveted cousin throne.*
*On my grandmother's lap with my*
*brother and cousin.*

M Y EARLIEST MEMORY is of me sitting on my grandmother's lap—maybe I was two or three, or maybe four or five, I really don't know. Her lap was a place I always felt safe on.

My grandmother was a storyteller. She painted images with her words. I am convinced if she had had a formal education, she would have been a writer. The amazing reservoir of her own life's tales, along with the vivid sense of imagination that she was gifted with, would have made such wonderful reading. Unfortunately for her, Russian was her first language, which she last studied when she was eight or so, and after moving to India when she was sixteen, she learned to speak some kind of broken English. By the time my cousins and I came along, she had come a long way, speaking not only English but also Hindi and Oriya, two Indian languages. I can only imagine what she would have done with a pen if she knew how to read and write.

As I grew older and more aware of the people around me, I used to watch my grandmother. She always seemed to be having long conversations with some unknown entity. Her head would turn this way and that, like she was facing and talking to people around her. The grim conversations would suddenly turn to a sad countenance; she would then retreat to her space, which was the easy chair on the verandah, with her hands folded on her lap.

She often sat there staring into the far distance, where one could not penetrate her thoughts. Her face went through countless expressions, sadness, pouting, conversations, pain, and anger. The conversations that she would have were in a different language. I never understood what she said. Sometimes, I think it was a language she created; by the time I came along, she had already spent almost sixty-five years in India and never spoke again the language she was born into. I do remember a few of the Russian lullabies she sang to put me to sleep, but she never spoke to any one of her children or grandchildren in Russian. So I do think she had forgotten her mother tongue.

Seeing her lost in her reverie, I could see her pain and loneliness more than ever. I must have been about six or so the first time I saw tears trickling down from those blue eyes, softly embedding themselves in the lines and crevices on her face, each line and each crevice with a story of their own to tell. I was in a corner on the verandah playing with my double-storied doll's house and my dolls when I turned around and saw all that sadness on her face.

Not very emotionally or verbally demonstrative even at that age, I remember sliding down the cemented red floor of the verandah to her and asking her why she was crying. "I miss my family. I don't know if I will ever see them again."

I am not sure I understood the significance of those words or the heaviness that was sitting in her heart. For me it was story time. As reluctant as she was to tell a story or, in her case, facts, she did open up her heart and her wounds. I think it was her way of staying connected with a part of her that was buried and fading. Maybe she thought by retelling this she would not lose her connection with her family.

( )

My grandmother was born and grew up in a village in the southeastern part of Russia where the tsar had ruled, near the Caucasus Mountain range in a little Azerbaijan town called Tiflis, now Tbilisi, the capital of Georgia.

My grandmother's name was Susember Rasho or Shushan Rasho. No one in the family is sure of her date and year of birth. We can only trace it back from the day my grandparents got married in Baghdad, on March 10, 1922. We think if she was fifteen, sixteen, or seventeen when she got married, she must have been born between 1905 and 1907. She was about four foot four inches and had typical Eurasian features. With light red hair, her eyes sometimes looked blue and sometimes green. She spoke with a lisp, and I sometimes think that might have been because of all the different languages she was exposed to in her journey from Russia to India. She never did know what language she needed to communicate in.

My grandmother would talk about how she grew up on this large property in a village right outside Tbilisi. Her father, who seemed to be some kind of chieftain or landlord, owned large tracts of land that were vineyards and orchards. She would talk about how they stored grapes from their vineyards, making wine and juices out of other fruits from their orchards.

She told us about horses and cattle and how she learned to ride a horse at a very early age. Reminiscing about her father's home, she recounted games of Hide-and-go-seek in the vineyards; she would lie down under the grapevines and eat the grapes directly from the vines. When the grapes were ready to be plucked, they would be gathered in heaps and put in large troughs. Then the jumping and crushing on the grapes would begin. Once they were crushed, the juice would be strained and put into vats along with kneaded dough, which helped with fermentation. This was also a time of celebration with singing and folk dances.

The one song that she carried with her and sang to all her seven children and me, was *Akshi Nanunen Shushan, Viskey madnekhad nishen, parch khardujam, dur danagan, deelam deelam, akshi nanunen shushan.* She could never explain the meaning of the entire song to us, other than her name, Shushan. She could never tell us what language it was, either.

Later in life, we thought it could have been a cross between Russian and Armenian. We will never know. The song will never die. I carry it with me.

Over and over, she would talk about the farm or the land she grew up in. It was mostly about how they rode horses almost all day long. I think this gave her a sense of freedom that she did not seem to have any more. It gave her a sense of power. She would tell us about how they would get on their horses and gallop away through the vast fields, riding through neighbors' orchards and fields, feeling the chill wind blow across their faces.

She talked about how she and her young siblings accompanied their father through many countries (I think because the Soviet Union was so large, every place they travelled to seemed like another country. Or she could have gone to other countries, and just did not remember where).

She would talk about the snow and how they played outside and all the snow people they built. They were always making soldiers in the snow, she said. Maybe in their young minds, they had already sensed a danger looming large on the horizon. The way she talked about her father and his travels, it seemed that he did some kind of conflict resolution. He knew both Russian and English, and always seemed to be called upon to settle some kind of skirmish or other.

She never talked about going to school or studying. My mother's two older sisters have documented some of my grandmother's history, but even there, there is no mention of any kind of education. I am not sure if her children ever asked her if she ever went to school, and I never asked.

Maybe with both her parents gone at such a young age, and having been raised by an Aunt Cruella, she never did get an opportunity to go to school. This is another fact that we will never know. I carry this regret with me every day. How, I wish, I could have talked to her more, asked her questions, gotten to know her life and most importantly, her feelings. Feelings were something you were not allowed to show or express when I was growing up.

My grandmother's family life, even in the early years, was a sad one. She and her two siblings had lost their mother at a young age—in childbirth while trying to bring her fourth child into the world. Their uncle's wife raised the little baby boy, who died under mysterious circumstances when he was two.

The skirmishes between East Germany, Europe, and the rise of the Bolsheviks in Russia were impacting their lives in major and tragic ways. Their father, who was always away, had left his three children with the cousin and his wife. The couple, who were childless, took them in, but the wife, my grandmother's aunt, turned out to be an unhappy and cruel person. She treated the siblings badly, never giving them enough food, sending them out in cold to gather wood for the fire, and always scolding them for something or other. Stories that I had only read in.

One day, not able to take her aunt's taunts and abuse, my grandmother spoke her mind. The cruel aunt, who was near the stove, took a hot spatula or some kind of kitchen object that was hot and singed my grandmother's scalp. Years and years later, as an adult, I still saw the pain in my grandmother's eyes when she would look into a mirror and tie that

scarf on her head whenever she went out or whenever someone came to visit.

My grandmother's father met a tragic end. As the turmoil
in the Soviet Union was getting closer and closer to home,
he would keep vigil against intruders, and one day was shot
in the head and killed. Once the skirmishes grew into full
blown fights, the people in the surrounding areas, including
my grandmother and her extended family, were moved from
village to village, eventually to safer countries controlled by
the British. Large populations were shifted to the East, to
Iran, Iraq, and India. In India, you still find offshoots of
Armenian and Russian families who emigrated during all
that turmoil.

My grandmother remembered the Russian Revolution
and World War I and how they had suffered through it.
When most of her family and relatives had gotten separated,
were killed, or had died along their trek to escape, she would
talk about how they gradually had to abandon whatever little belongings they had because it was getting too heavy to
carry. They ultimately became poor refugees living in tents
waiting to be resettled somewhere safe.

With great sorrow, she would talk about her older sister,
Rapka, who must have been around thirteen to my grandmother's eleven or twelve. Not wanting to take responsibility
for an almost-grown teenager, the uncle and aunt decided to
leave Rapka with a set of grandparents that were too old to
undertake the journey; those grandparents would keep her
safe from the marauding and looting crowds they might have
to face until she was married and sent off to her in-laws. That
was the last my eleven- or twelve-year-old grandmother saw

of her sister. She was now the sole protector of her younger brother, Nicholai, who they called Nicco for short. Nicco was nine or ten.

She talks about how she and her brother rode on horseback through the night and strayed from their relatives, how she consoled Nicco and how they kept riding, trying to find a familiar face in the exodus that seemed to be swelling with each step. Looking for someone known and familiar, they also saw dead people and horses lying in the snow, people and animals that were unable to take the stress and the burden of what was happening to them. I don't think she ever knew how long that escape took, or how long they stayed at the camp.

Heartbreak was not over for her as yet. A few years later, at the camp, once Nicco became older, maybe twelve or thirteen, he disappeared. My grandmother was heartbroken and devastated. Not knowing where he went, or how to look for him amidst all these strangers in a new land, she resolved herself to her fate of being alone in this world with no family or no one familiar close to her. I remember asking her years and years later, almost sixty years later, about her brother and sister. She had no idea whether anyone was still alive, and if so, on which continent they were.

She could not recount or tell us the number of years she spent at the Red Cross refugee camp in Baghdad. With all her family gone and feeling bereft and lonely, she threw herself into her work at the camp and did not think about what the future held for her. Her evenings were spent at the prayer meetings held at the fellowship hall in the camp. Growing up in an Orthodox Russian household, even though she spent just but a few years there, my grandmother was deeply religious and prayed every day. She prayed, she said, to the Almighty for a miracle. I am not sure what miracle she asked for, but I am sure she prayed every single day to be united with her family.

After spending a couple of months at the camp, my grandmother was relocated by the head nurse at the camp to go stay with a young Armenian couple and help out with household chores. She was to continue working at the Red Cross Hospital and at the camp. She seemed to be settling into her new routine, but heartbreak set in again. The young couple had gotten their papers to migrate to the United States, and were leaving Baghdad. Having nowhere to go, my grandmother found herself back at the refugee camp. The head nurse at the camp was a young British lady who took her under her wing once again. After another few months, one night, the head nurse sent for my grandmother.

"Sit down, my dear," she said. "There is good news and bad news for you."

"Are you sending me away again?"

"I called you because there is a marriage proposal for you."

"I don't want to get married to anyone. I want to stay here with you at the camp."

"You can't stay here forever. The war is over. I will be going back to England. Who will look after you? You have no relatives here. The man who wants to marry you is young and good-looking and is from India. He seems to be a decent young man who came here as a soldier."

My grandmother was frightened. "I don't want to marry him. I don't know him. I don't know where India is, and I don't know how to speak a foreign language. Please take me with you; take me to England with you and I will do all the work in your home for you."

The head nurse looked at her with tears in her eyes, and said, "I wish I could, but my country will not give me permission to take you with me. I promise I will find out everything about this young man before you get married. At least he is a Christian and comes from a country that is ruled by the British."

My grandmother fled the room weeping. The head nurse sat, thinking about my grandmother's insecure life and how best to help her. But after going to the head of the YMCA and asking them to do a background check on my grandfather, there was little else she could do.

A few weeks later, the head of the YMCA received papers about the Samal family in Cuttack from the Pastor of the Baptist Church. It seems the family was highly regarded and possessed several acres of land with tenants. They were also regular churchgoers. The head nurse at the camp scrutinized the papers, explaining them to Susember, and showing her a map of the world and pointing out where India was.

My grandmother stopped fighting the proposal. She realized she had nowhere to go other than to make a radical change. Any hopes of reuniting with her family had long been buried after living at the refugee camp for years. She realized she needed shelter more than anything else. If it meant marrying a stranger, then that is what she would do.

# 2
# *Marriage*

❨ ❩

*My grandparents on their wedding day,*
*March 10, 1922, in Baghdad, Iraq.*

E.B. SAMUEL AND SUSEMBER (SUSAN) RASHO got married at the camp with the head nurse and the head of the YMCA standing in as parents. The couple settled in a small house in Baghdad while my grandfather continued his work with the YMCA. Emotionally and mentally, my grandmother had a wide chasm to cross. While he was at work during the day, she would cry her heart out for her circumstances. She would keep reminding herself that she was a Rasho and Rashos were of a stronger stock and she could never give up.

Trying to keep her mind and hands busy, she tried to make their house into a home, cooking whatever little she knew from her camp days and the days she spent with the Armenian couple. My grandfather would praise and relish everything she made, and he gradually began teaching her some spoken English. They would communicate in Arabic, which she was more comfortable and adept with than my grandfather after staying in the camp for all those years.

She called him *Khunnu*, which is the Arabic word for brother, since that was what all the people who worked at the Y were called, and he called her *Puttu*, which in Oriya, my grandfather's native language, meant little person, since she was so petite. They would talk about their families and how they both had gotten to Baghdad. He would share with her his dreams for his career back home and how he would build them a home on his ancestral property and how they would always have a permanent shelter. All this sounded safe and grounded to my grandmother. It raised her hopes for her future and the yearning to call some place home at last.

After living for a few months in Baghdad, my grandfather got information about a ship that was going to be leaving for India in a few weeks. He bought two tickets for passage to Bombay, India. Susember was excited about travelling by sea for the first time in her life, but still worried about the land she was going to and the people who lived there. Knowing that my grandfather had family in India brought her some kind of solace, but it also left her anxious about how accepting they would be of a foreigner. Would they accept her children as Indians? All these thoughts bothered her, especially since she was expecting her first child. Without a job, how would they raise their child? She tried to put these thoughts out of her mind as she began the tedious process of wrapping up another chapter of her life.

The ship that they boarded was crowded. Most of the people on the ship had the same story with shared experiences. They were all refugees, expressing the same concern and sorrows: of being uprooted, the loss of home and country, and the insecurity of going into the unknown. Everyone spoke a different language with a smattering of English to understand and be understood by others. All this, in a weird way, made Susember feel not so isolated. It comforted her that there were hundreds like her who were starting life anew in unknown destinations. She just prayed that her husband's family would be accepting and loving of her.

The ship eventually docked in Bombay (Mumbai, now). For my grandfather, he was excited. He was home. For my grandmother, there was trepidation about the unknown future. From Bombay, train tickets were bought for both of them to travel to Cuttack. After an arduous three-day journey, through which my grandmother saw a whole different fascinating world through the train windows—of hawkers on the platforms, noise and color everywhere—they reached Cuttack. They arrived at a tiny station that was lit by a dingy lantern. The fog outside made for low visibility. Susember could barely see anything or anyone.

The first shock she got was when the coolie walked up to them to pick up their luggage. She noticed his mouth and lips were blood red and that he was chewing on something. In fear, she exclaimed, "These people eat human beings!" Laughing out loud, my grandfather explained reassuringly that what they were eating was not human beings, but *paan*, which is a betel leaf filled with condiments. To prove his point, he walked up to the paan vendor, bought a paan, put it in his mouth, and showed her it wasn't a human being. This was the beginning of all the culture shocks she would start experiencing.

At the station in Cuttack, my grandfather's excitement knew no bounds. He was home and he was home with a new wife and he was home with a new wife who was a foreigner. The coolie walked them outside to a horse-drawn carriage, which my grandfather explained was because the British had these conveyances made like they had in England.

"We are going to the home of one of my cousins now, where we will stay for a couple of weeks while I attend to my land business and apply for a job."

The buggy clattered along dusty roads while they rode through streets that had no streetlights. A few shops were open here, and they were all dimly lit by candles or lanterns. They passed by the land where my grandfather's ancestral home once stood, the Baptist Church where he told her they would attend services on Sunday, and the only European school in Cuttack where the British taught and where their children would go to school.

When they were nearing his cousin's home, my grandfather taught my grandmother how to fold her hands and say

*Namaskar*, or *Namaste*, the way Indians greeted each other. He also told her about the age-old tradition of touching the feet of older relatives in a gesture of asking for their blessings.

All these new traditions and culture were doing nothing to assuage my grandmother of the great nervousness she felt. The food had already been a shock to her and her system. She had no idea what she had eaten either on the train or at the various stops at different platforms on her three-day journey. She was hungry and anxious.

Arriving at his cousin's home and jumping out of the buggy even before it came to a halt, my grandfather started banging on the large wooden door of this house that had a straw roof. My grandmother looked at the thatched roof in bewilderment, wondering what kind of people lived under there. She had never seen a home with a thatched roof before.

Rushing in, my grandfather, who went back to being called Bidyut (the name he was born with), greeted all his long-lost relatives with hugs, kisses, and a lot of touching of feet. Everyone talked in Oriya and kept throwing out barrages of questions; they had not seen him in ten years or so. Since my grandmother could not communicate verbally with them, they hugged her, pinched her pink cheeks since she was so fair, and rolled their hands through her red hair. Other than seeing British missionaries on the street or teaching at local schools, none of my grandfather's family had seen a foreigner up close and personal. To them, she was a novelty.

The next day, my grandfather left my grandmother in the care of his cousins and their family and went about trying to sort out his business and work. While she stayed home, she was bombarded with questions about what she was, where she came from, and how did she meet my grandfather. A few of the girl cousins were in college, so the conversations in English were not too difficult. She was happy that she seemed to have been accepted wholeheartedly by her husband's family.

In her quiet moments, she would think about the world she had left behind, particularly her childhood days in her own land and with her own community before the quiet was ripped apart by the turmoil. Then she would think about her life as a refugee and the years she lived at the Red Cross Camp. She would wonder about how she had the courage to accept a husband from a totally strange land, to live with him and to trust him to lead her wherever he went. Sometimes, she said, she questioned her sanity. She barely knew the man she had married. His culture and hers were miles apart.

They were two strangers trying to make a home and start a family together. Moments like this, she would be filled with remorse and sadness and would burst into tears in her room. Her heart would cry out for her beloved family and country. Feeling weak and helpless, she tended to become withdrawn.

When my grandfather came back from his daily endeavors to find work, he would find her depressed and sad. He tried to calm her down each time and answer her questions as best as he could. Each time, he tried to explain to her that it would take her a little time to settle in, to get used to being in a foreign land. He promised her that once she got used to the land, she would love it.

Being a young teenager, my grandmother felt comforted by his words, and started depending on him for almost everything. Even though he was only in his early twenties, my grandmother thought him to be wise and worldly. Her dependence on him was beginning to find strong roots. She seemed beholden to him in more ways than one. He asked her to be patient and told her that as soon as he started working, they would have their own home to live in. These days of feeling burdened in someone else's home would soon pass.

My grandfather's cousins took good care of her. They plied her with food, especially because she was pregnant. She still could not relish the strange, pungent food. The only thing that was familiar to her was the boiled rice, and this was the only thing she would eat. Not allowed to do housework like she did in their little home in Baghdad, all she did when she was not taking naps was sit on the verandah and wait for her husband to come home.

One day, he took her to meet his mother's family. The conservative Hindus that they were, they did not allow her to step into their home because she was white and was a Christian. My grandfather walked out of their home, never ever to return or to speak to them again.

The next few months rolled about the same way. My grandfather had applied to the Civil Services and had taken an entrance exam. They were waiting for his results. The Oriya way of life was beginning to grow on my grandmother. It was slow and all-encompassing.

With so many relatives to visit, they went from home to home to pay their respects and to introduce my grandmother to the family. They ate their way through homes, as is the Indian tradition. She blended in with everything, trying to please everyone, trying to feel accepted, but still not able to figure out what they really thought about her. After a while, the only thing that mattered to her was pleasing her husband, who kept prompting her about what was acceptable and what was not. She was grateful to him for his guidance.

A few months later, after their oldest son was born, my grandfather got the news that he had been appointed to the Secretariat Office in Patna, in the state of Bihar. They were overjoyed with the upward trend their lives were taking.

After moving to Patna and settling in with the new work and the new baby in yet another strange land with yet another different language spoken, life in a new city for the young couple seemed to take its toll. They argued about almost everything: the food to be eaten, the child-rearing. The language barrier they still faced, where she would say something, and mean or want something absolutely different, was rocking their marriage. My grandfather, it seems, was the patient partner, the understanding one, while she seemed to be impulsive and angry. He seemed to calm her on most days with his logic and by being the educated one and the gentler one.

One of my grandmother's lifelong regrets was not being able to read or write. There were days where she blamed my grandfather for not getting her a tutor or focusing on her ability to read or write so that she could help her children with their homework or even understand some of the things they would be saying. This may be the number one reason my grandmother always took a back seat to my grandfather and had a low profile when it came to making or taking major decisions in the family. Maybe she thought her lack of education was a hindrance and might lead to bad decisions.

As life ebbed and flowed with my grandparents, my grandfather was reaching heights in his career. He rose up to be the under-secretary of state. He was a self-made, self-educated man, extremely driven and ambitious. Much later in life, his official business letters where he communicated with the British Authorities were taught and shown as samples at the Indian Administrative Academy.

My grandmother, meanwhile, was settling into her role as a mother and as a government official's wife. With that came all the Durbar (Garden) Parties that she had to throw and attend. They started buying things for their home, an English bone china set and furniture, and setting up their home. My grandfather bought her a sewing machine, and she made curtains for their home, clothes for the children, and sometimes even his shirts. That sewing machine she still had with her when I was growing up. Sometimes she would sew my frocks and my concert costumes.

Their family had grown from two to six in a few years. The older two children were sent back to my grandfather's hometown, Cuttack, to study in that European school, the Stewart School. As it was a boarding school, they stayed in the dorm. It broke my grandmother's heart to be parted from her children, but once again, I think she took a back seat and gave in to my grandfather, who wanted his children to be educated in a formal British school and setting. The couple returned to Patna with two children fewer and went back to their daily routine.

One evening, he returned from the office and told her that there were rumors flying about a second World War brewing between two old enemies, Germany and Britain, along with their World War I allies. Susember was extremely distressed to hear this. She wondered what all this would mean for India as a British colony. All her old fears returned: the search for new places, more refugees, more wounded soldiers, more recruitment of soldiers, and more deaths and dislocations. My grandfather tried to assuage her fears by saying, "These are just rumors; it may not develop into another World War. Don't worry." My grandmother threw herself into her growing family to keep her mind away from the ghosts of the past.

As he rose in his department professionally, with rumors of the war growing stronger and the British Raj (Kingdom) recruiting young men for the army once again, my grandfather was getting ready to be transferred back to his home state of Orissa to become the deputy under-secretary of the provincial cabinet. This move, they both seemed to love: my grandmother because it would mean being close to their children in boarding school, and my grandfather, other than rising in his career, because he would finally get that chance to build the home on his ancestral land that he had promised. My grandmother was then expecting her seventh child, my mother.

*My grandparents with six out of their seven children. The youngest girl standing on the right is my mother.*

# 3
# *Nicco*

《 》

I

N 1936, just a few days before my grandparents were getting ready to leave Patna for Cuttack, a strange letter arrived at my grandfather's office postmarked from Baghdad. It was from my grandmother's brother Nicholai.

My grandfather brought the letter home to my grandmother, who fainted when she saw it. Since she could not read, he read the letter out to her. Nicholai wrote about himself, explaining why he had disappeared from the camp. We learned later that he had to go underground because he had returned to his village in Russia to avenge his father's killing. During that time, taking revenge was common, and expected as a way to preserve your honor and settle scores among different clans. He enclosed a picture of himself and his bride, a pretty Armenian woman. He wrote saying he had gone back to the Red Cross Hospital in Baghdad and from the files there had found out where my grandmother had gone and got my grandfather's address. My grandfather, who was now deeply ensconced in the government, was easy to trace.

My grandmother could not believe that the little boy of twelve or thirteen was now this grown-up man with a wife. She wept with joy and wanted to go to Baghdad right away. But with seven children to care for, it did not seem possible for them to leave and go. My grandfather promised to work on getting Nicco and his wife, Azadoui, to come to India. He replied to Nicco, giving the address for the Secretariat in Cuttack, since they were getting ready to move back.

After settling into a rented home in Cuttack, my grandfather went back to work. My grandmother was home tending her seven children. When she was in the home by herself, and the kids were in school and her husband at work all the time, thoughts of the home that she had left, the father that she had known, and the mother that she had lost haunted her and waves of loneliness would sweep over her. She would try to put all her thoughts away, because she knew nothing from the past would ever come back, but the ghosts lingered.

When she went through these phases, she would stop doing whatever she was doing, go sit in a corner with her head in her hands, and talk to unseen people like she was having real-time conversations. The number of times I saw her do this while I was growing up was so many that when I close my eyes, even now, I see her in her housecoat, sitting on that cane chair, her scarf tied on her head. Her wrinkled hands had faint tattoos on one hand, which was where they were marked before they left their home, little symbols to signify their village.

Outside their world, the Second World War had begun. By 1939, the war had escalated. As the war raged in Europe, people in India, including my grandparents and their children, tried to go on with their lives as usual. However, with India being a British colony, the reverberations were felt; someone had a soldier son missing, or someone's backyard where they were getting ready to bury yet another brave Indian soldier. Tears, uncertainty, and loss flowed freely everywhere.

The British government, meanwhile, was busy separating the Indian Provinces, drawing lines and creating new states. The divide and conquer rule, is what the Indians called it.

So the seven children grew up in the midst of privilege and pride. They loved being children of a mixed couple. My grandfather had bought a Ford convertible and all seven of the kids were packed in there with their parents to go out on picnics, to the movies, or just to have a fun time in general. The convertible would be followed by a jeep with attendants who would be carrying food and drinks for the picnics. I guess with the seven of them to play with each other, they did not really need friends. We grandkids, at a much later date, would be regaled by stories of their escapades.

Meanwhile, my grandparent's home was nearing completion. My grandfather named it "Moti Bhavan": *Moti* (meaning pearl, his mother's first name) and *Bhavan*, meaning home. The final touches of the two pillars for the gate were done. The marble plaques for the gate were installed, the one on the left reading "E. B. Samuel," and the one on the right, "Moti Bhavan." Years later, every time I walked through those wrought iron gates my sense of pride knew no bounds.

*Moti Bhavan, the home that my grandfather built.*

As soon as the family moved into their own new home, the air raid signals and practices for the war began. My grandfather's work increased. He had to tour frequently to acquaint the public with news about the war. He would announce this from an official government jeep with a microphone in his hand, telling the people what they needed to do when the signals sounded. Trenches were being dug up wherever needed. Town hall–type meetings were being held to prepare for the worst. War clouds hovered all over India. Young men were enlisting and leaving for shores and destinations unknown, and some of them were protecting the Indian borders for the British Empire. However, Orissa, being so far away from important outposts and targets, was relatively safe.

Peace was shattered in the Samuel household when the oldest child, Charles, who was seventeen, enlisted in the army. My grandfather, it seemed, was at some level proud that a son of his was following in his soldier footsteps. For my grandmother, this was earth-shattering. It was a reminder once again of the trauma she had endured. All she wanted to do was protect her family from a destiny such as hers. There was nothing she could do. Her son was independent and wanted to make decisions about his own life. All she could do was pray.

Once Charles joined the military academy, he wrote home occasionally to give updates of what was going on. My grandmother had to rely on the six other children to read his letters to her and give her newspaper updates. I just cannot imagine how helpless she must have felt. I cannot imagine not being able to read or write or communicate with the world.

Life continued for the Samuels, albeit with a cloud always hovering over their heads. Their safe family unit of nine had been disrupted by the world and events beyond their control. E.B. Samuel and Susember continued life in the government milieu. My aunts used to talk about how my grandmother would go to these parties dressed up in her finery with high heels, a long gold and amber chain around her neck, and a gold armlet. She would return from the tea parties with funny observations about the English Memsahibs (British Society Ladies). This strikes me both as funny and poignant, and goes to show how assimilated she had become with the land and the culture that was India, forgetting that she herself was a Foreign Memsahib in the country.

Much later in life, when I became part of the landscape in Cuttack, I remember her being addressed by people close to the family as "Belaiti (foreign) Mummy," and by acquaintances as "Belaiti Memsahib." If one goes back to Cuttack today and asks someone about the Belaiti Memsahib, they would direct you to where our home was.

My grandfather was now Under Secretary in the Home Department of the Secretariat. The Quit India movement against the British was gaining traction, and in 1940, the British had started holding round table conferences to confer on the possibility of allowing India to take over ruling their own country. News of rumblings in Europe about an imminent war and the stirring of Nationalist feelings in Indians were at the forefront. Through all this, my grandfather was trying to get Nicco and his family out of Baghdad and to India. Then World War II broke out, and contact with Nicco and his family was again lost. A broken heart once again my grandmother nursed.

The war ended in 1945. After bloodshed, chaos, and the splitting of a sovereign nation into two separate countries based on religion, India and Pakistan, the British finally left India in August of 1947.

A few months before India gained its independence from the British, my oldest aunt, my grandparent's second born, sailed to London to study. Since India was in such a chaotic state, she decided to take her Uncle Nicco's letter and pictures with her to England to see if she would have a better chance of tracing him and establishing contact. All the children had seen and knew what their mother had gone through and how she longed to find her family. In their own ways, they did whatever they could to help. With Europe being in such turmoil and trying to rebuild after the war, she did not have much luck. She returned to India, completing her degree after a couple of years.

In 1960, she went back to London, this time to work, and once again took the letters and the picture with her and promised her mother she would not come back till she had found her uncle. She did keep her promise. She never found her uncle; she never came back to India. In 1961, she passed away in London, a young girl of twenty-three, a few days after giving birth to a baby. Along with her life, her belongings, and everything else including the last known address of Nicco, everything was gone. Her ashes were flown back to India, and along with burying her child, my grandmother buried her longings to meet her family.

No one spoke about it in the family anymore. The remaining six children were all grown with families of their own. Dora, the third child and daughter of my grandparents, had married a German engineer in India and had moved with him in the late 1950s to Berlin. Settling into her new life there, she never forgot her mother's angst. In the late sixties, she started her search for her uncle once again. Going to the Red Cross office in Berlin, she asked for help to dig through the old files. She did not find anything, but never gave up hope.

# 4

# *Nicco and Rapka*

❰ ❱

I N 1974 a West German radio program started a new segment of announcing daily the names of people that were lost during both wars. At the end of the program, they gave an address for their headquarters in Munich for people to write in about their lost ones. My Aunt Dora reached out to the Red Cross, which was supporting the segment, with Nicholai Rasho's information and last known address. After trying for two years to locate him, the Red Cross finally gave up and wrote to my aunt saying the Middle East arm of the Red Cross, which was called the Red Crescent, was not replying to their queries.

Not one to give up easily, Dora thought out of the box, and came to the conclusion that maybe they were not responding to the Red Cross because the letters were in German and no one was willing to make an effort to get them translated. She took matters into her own hands, and wrote to the director of the Red Crescent directly, one copy in English and one in Arabic, which she got a friend to write.

Exactly a month later, in August of 1976, she received an unsigned, typed letter from her uncle Nicco. Her joy knew no bounds, yet she was apprehensive. So many years had gone by, and so many events had unfolded. How could she be sure this was really her uncle? Several weeks later while at work, she received a call. The operator said it was from East Germany. Not knowing anyone on the other side of the wall, she was a little bewildered but took the call anyhow.

A gentle male voice on the other side asked, "Dora?"

"Yes?"

"Dora, you know your Uncle Nicholai? I am a near and dear friend of his. My name is Wanik Gabodian, and I have come from Baghdad. I have a message for you from your uncle. When can I come see you?"

Dora nearly collapsed in shock. She replied, "TODAY!"

"No, not today, but sometime next week, as I have some business in East Berlin."

The week went by in agony for my aunt. She still did not know, after so many disappointments, whether this man was for real and whether he would show up. When the doorbell rang in her flat on the appointed day, out there on the landing stood this man with a box of chocolates in his hand, the first living bridge between her and her mother's brother. It seems when Wanik saw her, he was astounded to see the close resemblance between her and Nicco's daughter. "Yes, you are your uncle's niece. Very much so!"

Wanik had brought with him pictures of Nicco and his family, and she recognized him from the picture that he had sent to them in India in 1952. Apparently, Nicco had changed his last name from Rasho to Azin and had been living in Baghdad after the war with his family. His two sons, Sargon and Daud,(Daniel now) had immigrated to the United States and were living in Chicago.

Wanik still had another surprise up his sleeve for my aunt. "Did you know you have an aunt called Rapka in Russia?"

"Yes, of course," my aunt answered.

"Well, she has been trying to locate her lost family, her younger sister and younger brother," said Wanik. He went on to explain that my grandmother's sister had been looking for my grandmother and her brother, Nicholai. Rapka somehow found out about some people who had been with my grandmother at the refugee camp back in 1917, and got her address in India. The story those people told Rapka nearly knocked her off her chair: The strangers and Uncle Shaul and his family were neighbors in Tehran. Rapka had come back home with Uncle Shaul's address, and had written to him immediately, asking him if he knew where Susember and Nicco were.

Even though my grandmother and Nicco got separated from Shaul during the exodus, Nicco, after becoming an adult and because he was still in that same region, had reestablished contact with his uncle and stayed in touch. Uncle Shaul sent Rapka his address, and just a few days before Wanik had to leave for Germany, Rapka's letter arrived at

Nicco's. Wanik had brought that along with him for my aunt. Within days, my aunt was writing to Rapka with pictures of the family in India.

Meanwhile, she started planning on how to get Nicco and his wife to visit India. The year was late 1976 when all this transpired. In January 1977, my aunt got her first letter from Rapka. Rapka wrote to say that she did not know whether to cry or to laugh. She wrote about her family and all that they had gone through over the years. The letter echoed and reflected what my grandmother had felt across a different continent on the other side of the world. There was so much pain in each of their stories and lives. Rapka had enclosed a picture of herself, and my aunt was not shocked at all to see the close resemblance. They could have been the same person. Fate plays such cruel games and is full of such comedies and tragedies.

It was time to break the news to my grandparents, especially my grandmother, and the rest of the family in India. My aunt did not want to give any false hope to my grandmother, who had already suffered such tremendous loss. The day she broke the news I still remember. We never had a telephone at home while I was growing up. The downstairs portion of our home was rented out to an office on one side and the resident manager of the office lived in the other half with his family. They had a telephone. That evening in mid-January, a voice boomed out from downstairs, "Trunk Call!" When that happened, my grandparents and I would always run down because it would have to be an overseas call either from my aunt in Germany or my uncle in Australia. Sure enough, it was my aunt from Germany.

As usual, it was my grandfather who would pick up the phone to talk. When he did, my aunt asked him to give my grandmother the phone. Always reluctant to talk on the phone because she was getting hard of hearing, my grandmother nevertheless got on the phone.

To make sure her mother heard her, my aunt's voice boomed, "Mumma! Mumma, I found Nicco. I found Uncle Nicco!" Even I heard that.

My grandmother kept her gaze steady and didn't say a word. I have no idea what she was feeling, or even if she had heard her daughter.

Seeing my grandmother not react, my grandfather took the phone from her and asked, "Dora, what are you saying?"

"Daddy, Uncle Nicco and his wife, Azadoui, are flying to India in February. I have already booked their tickets and organized their travel. You will need to go to Calcutta to pick them up."

"Puttu," that was the first time in my sixteen years I had heard my grandfather use the term of endearment. "Did you hear what Dora said? They are coming, Nicco and his wife."

I have never seen my grandmother cry the way she did that evening. All her love, sorrow, anguish, and pain seemed to flow out in tsunami proportions. No one slept that night. Our downstairs tenants celebrated with us.

After that, the frenzied activity of preparing for their arrival started. The house was painted and whitewashed. Linen, curtains, and comforters were all bought new. The food was planned out. It was decided that my grandmother would stay home with me since I had school, and so my grandfather left by himself for Calcutta to bring them to our hometown.

My grandfather brought the couple home by train from Calcutta and arrived at home early one morning. The scene that morning at our home was unforgettable. Nicco stepped out of the Rickshaw in front of our house along with his wife, Azo. Looking on from my upstairs window, it was like seeing a male version of my grandmother. The stocky Russian build, the same shuffling, slow walk, and up close I saw his eyes, eyes that had seen and felt a lot. Yet hope shone in them. They were the same blue-green as my grandmother's eyes.

My grandmother, who was usually a late riser, was awake and dressed and waiting at the gate, the same gates that she had walked into with her young family, with no hopes of ever seeing her family again. But here she was, almost seventy years later, waiting for a little eight-year-old boy she had taken charge of when she was ten or twelve.

Nicco got off the rickshaw and had eyes only for his sister. With tears streaming down his face, he engulfed her in one huge bear hug. I can only imagine my grandmother's emotions. After all those years, finally looking and touching someone who belonged to the same soil as you. Someone who had everything in common with you but had lived a life so far away.

After all those years separating them, it was like they picked up where they had left off. They were safe, together, with nothing to fear. The only tragedy was they could not communicate. My grandmother had forgotten Russian, and Nicco knew no English. Azo, who was Armenian, knew a smattering of English, and with her help and hand gestures, they managed to communicate. Blood, like they say, needs no language. My aunt had still not told my grandmother or any one of us that Rapka was in Russia and had been found too. She wanted Nicco to be the one to break that news to her.

*This is me with my grandparents when Nicco and Rapka came to India in 1977.*

After breakfast, Nicco and Azo were given a tour of the house and our garden. My grandmother walked them through every event of her life like she was trying to make up for lost time and include them in her life. That afternoon, the four adults and I gathered as usual on our verandah, which was where most relaxed social tête-à-têtes in our household happened. Nicco brought out his travel bag and pulled out an envelope that had a letter and some pictures. He showed my grandmother the pictures, and asked my grandmother if she knew who that was.

She did not even need a second. "Rapka!"

"Yes, yes," Nicco kept nodding his head.

Brother and sister were once again engulfed in tears. Azo was clutching her heart, crying and saying something in Armenian. Emotions that day were everywhere. Even my grandfather, the stoic, strong-hearted one, broke down crying. I was busy taking pictures with my little broken camera.

After spending two months in India, travelling to different parts to see family, Nicholai and Azadoui headed back to Baghdad. The parting of the brother and sister was heartbreaking. Both of them were getting older, and they knew this might be the last time. The only gratifying thought was that they had finally met again, and at least no longer had that unknown fear in their minds.

Meanwhile, the process had begun to have my grandmother, who had never left India after she set foot in it in the 1920s, fly to Russia to meet her sister. With Russia not being an easy country to travel into, my grandmother's passport, visa, and other necessary documents took two years. They finally came through in 1980. My grandmother was about seventy-five years old.

My grandmother and my Aunt Nora flew into Donetsk on April 31, 1980. Almost sixty-three years after she had left, my grandmother got off that plane, and with her rickety knees, bent down and kissed her motherland.

Time stood still. It seemed the entire airport at Donetsk was filled with the village. Rapka, who had lost her husband a while ago, stood waiting at the large glass window with her thirteen children, grandchildren, and extended family. There was no place to move or breathe. Those were the days of getting off the plane and walking on the tarmac and through a set of doors. Everything was visible both from the outside and inside once you walked off the plane.

My aunt realized for the first time what my grandmother must have gone through not seeing the faces of her own people for over six decades. Everywhere Nora looked, peering out of the airport windows, were faces that reflected her mother's face. There was no doubt that this was home, and that this was where my grandmother truly belonged.

*My grandmother and her sister Rapka in Donestk, Russia, in 1980.*

My grandmother walked through those airport doors, and the two sisters flew into each other's arms, sobbing and both speaking in a language neither understood. But once again, love and blood needed no language.

After spending a month and a half with her sister in Donetsk, it was time for my grandmother to head back. As the day drew closer, she became quiet and anxious. It seems she would sit outside the house and just smell the air. Maybe she was trying to feel her father's essence and was trying to capture it in her heart to take back with her. Maybe she smelt the horses she had grown up with. Not one for being very verbal, especially about her own emotions, I will never really know her thoughts.

Again, the day the sisters parted was heartbreaking. Physically, they had met, but still the lack of a common language kept them apart. Imagine if they had shared a language. Imagine the stories of heartbreak, joy, and sorrow the sisters would have shared. Imagine the secrets they would have told each other.

The sweet and sorrowful parting of the sisters came with a hope that one day the three siblings would meet together under one roof. Today, as I sit here and write, I can report that the meeting never happened. Age and fate intervened. Rapka was closing in on eighty and was not in the best of health to travel, and Nicco and his wife immigrated to America. My grandmother, who a few months after her trip to Russia broke her hip, was also not fit to travel. And so my grandmother settled back into her routine.

# PART II

Preface

It was on the 6th anniversary of the birthday of my child Bubu (Shabnam Singh) that I was seized with two ideas, viz (i) to start a photo album containing her photographs from her birth, and (ii) to write, in a letter form, all events, connected with her life. My intention is that in the peculiar circumstances in which she is now placed, Bubu ought to know everything when she is in a position to understand and shift matters for herself. She ought not to be ignorant of her life since birth - when she comes to the proper age.

As I have been watching over her growth from birth my mind is getting filled with anxieties for her future. I am growing old and with it my love

*The first page from the notebook my grandfather documented my life in.*

# 5

# The Diary

( )

*It was on the 6th anniversary of the birthday of my child Bubu (Shabnam Singh) that I was seized with two ideas, viz (i) to start a photo album containing her photographs from her birth and (ii) to write, in a letter form, all events, connected with her life. My intention is that in the peculiar circumstances in which she is now placed, Bubu ought to know everything when she is in a position to understand and shift matters for herself. She ought not to be ignorant of her life since birth—when she comes to the proper age.*

THIS BOOK. More like an epistolary, I would watch my grandfather write in it, alone in his room, lying back in his easy chair with a makeshift clipboard to base this notebook on and a red pen in hand. Yes, a fountain pen. He had bottles of blue, red, and black inks on his desk, sitting between his Bible and his typewriter.

Everything he did was precise and methodical. His routines were the same every single day of his life. From getting up at 4:30 A.M. every morning, sitting in his redone and refurbished car seat on the verandah (not a baby car seat, but the real one), to singing hymns and stropping his razor blade, to going downstairs to feed the chickens at 5:00 and methodically going about his day, which was no different than the day before or the day that would come after, till he sat down at 7:30 P.M. after dinner to pick up the book and write in it, everything was the same.

Something about the way he went about it, writing in the book, I knew it was not something he would tell me or talk to me about. Somehow, I knew it was about me. I knew it was about me because of the way things were. Every time I walked into my grandfather's room, if his cupboard was open, he would immediately close it. But not before the curious, prying eyes of a six year old scoped out what was in there, filing it at the back of my head, the position of the book, the files underneath it, and the direction it faced. The cupboard was always locked when he was not around.

The earliest memories I have of my grandfather must have been when I was five or six. He was a tall, lean, six-foot Indian who wore top hats and safari suits or business suits during the day, and a *dhoti* and *kurta* (an Indian form of male formal attire) in the evenings when he went out for a walk. On most days, I would be summoned to go with him on those walks. It was a time where I would be told I was not studying hard enough, not walking straight enough, or that I was swinging my hands a bit too much while I walked. Yet, he loved me.

My grandfather was possessive and controlling. I was never allowed to have friends over, never allowed to have sleepovers with my cousins, never allowed to go out with family friends. "Your cousins are going out of town and asked if you could go with them. But how can I let you go and make my house dark by your absence?" There were so many Nevers. Yet, yet he loved me.

We, the three of us, my grandfather, my grandmother and I, lived in a beautiful two-storied brick and mortar home. This home was designed by my grandfather's cousin, whom he called Ranchu (Ranchur Jee Jachuck). This was the same cousin he cofounded the YMCA with, and they remained connected all their lives. We had five bedrooms upstairs and six bedrooms downstairs, not to mention the sprawling drawing rooms both upstairs and downstairs and the large dining rooms and open gardens all around us. I loved our home because I loved how big it was, and because it signified we were well to do and belonged to an upper-class society. To my child's mind, that was very important. Especially to a child who had nothing else to show off.

I was born in April of 1961. In October of 1963, my mother wrote to my grandfather and told him that he needed to come to Delhi and bring me away, and if he did not, she would give me away or put me in an orphanage.

Dispensable is what I was. A girl child in India does not bring much value to the family. She was, and still is, a responsibility. There is no point in educating her much, because eventually she will be in her husband's home. The family needs to make sure she is sent to her husband's home with a collection of good saris, new pots and pans of a good quality that she can cook in for her husband and in-laws, and the latest refrigerator, oh yes, where she can make all the ice cream she wants, showing off to her in-laws the skills she learned at a neighborhood cooking class. Not to mention the gold jewelry that they would need to invest in for her marriage. Such a waste of investment this would be, with no returns for the future.

In her letter to her father, my mother gave no reason except that she and my father were separating and that she needed to find a job to fend for herself. It seems my father had already left, taking my brother, Pintu, who was almost seven, with him. My grandfather wrote back to my mother to have her bring me to Cuttack, their home.

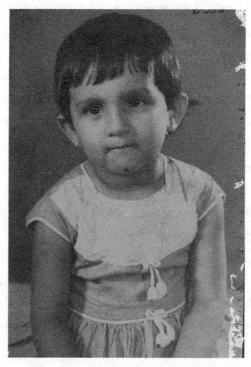

*My official picture from the orphanage in New Delhi, India.*

Impatient as she was to jump-start her new life, my mother did not have the patience to wait for my grandfather's letters to arrive. She went ahead and put me in an orphanage. No one in our family talks about this. On November 19, 1963, I was sent to the orphanage. I was two years and eleven months old. I am thankful for my official admittance picture from the orphanage that my grandfather kept for me. It allowed me to patch my story together.

By the time my grandfather's letter arrived, telling my mother that no grandchild of his would be raised in an orphanage, it was January of 1964. I am presuming that once she got the letter, she must have gone back and asked to take me back. My mother wrote back saying she did not have the time to travel to Cuttack and would be putting me on a plane from New Delhi to Calcutta (Kolkata now), which was an overnight train journey, almost eight hours away from my grandfather's home. Yes, she put a not even turned three year old on a plane.

My almost seventy-year-old grandfather set out immediately. It did not matter that he was going straight into communal riots that had broken out in Calcutta between Hindus and Muslims and might not have been safe. On the fourteenth of January, 1964, my grandfather arrived at the Dum Dum Airport in Calcutta, way before the plane was scheduled to arrive at 9:00 A.M.. As the arrival time of the plane got closer, and went by, and there was still no plane, his anxiety level increased. Finally, he was told that the plane I was on had caught fire shortly after takeoff and had been forced to land in a different city. In a time where there were not many communication infrastructures, he had no idea how I was or where I was.

Eight hours after the scheduled arrival time, the plane finally landed. My grandfather stood at the bottom of the airplane's ramp. Once the doors opened and people started trickling out, a stewardess walked out with me in her arms, bawling my head off and crying, "Mummy, Mummy." Even though the stewardess did not know who my grandfather was, she handed me over to him because as soon as he saw me, he called out to me, "Bubuni," the name he had used for me for the first two years of my life. I stopped crying immediately and jumped into his arms.

As I understand it, the people getting off the plane stopped my grandfather and told him their lives had been saved because of me. That God could not allow anything to happen to a plane that had a little angel on it. It was all over the newspapers the next day.

> By bus we came to the air office and there I took a taxi, which brought us to the friend's house in Howrah, before 6 P.M. You were crying all the time. I was told that you had not eaten on the plane. After reaching their house, I fed you and put you on the commode. While I had gone to bring something from the other room you fell down from the commode and hurt yourself. After I had given you a wash, I fed you some dinner. All the time you were crying for your mother. My heart was breaking. What cursed parents you had.

My grandmother, when all this was transpiring—my journey from my parents home to the orphanage to my grandaprent's home—was visiting one of her sons in a different city. With no telephone service easily available in those days, she had no idea of what was going on. Once she came back home, she was surprised to see me there. My grandmother, who had always deferred back to my grandfather when it came to tough and important decisions, had once again no contribution or say in what needed to be done.

Their roles had been clearly defined in the early years of their marriage. My grandfather, with his education, the power to read and write, and experience, was clearly the stronger one of the two in terms of the outside world and the future. My grandmother's role was to tend to home and hearth and make sure it was comfortable and safe for the children.

So when the time came for my grandfather to come rescue me, he just did what he had to. Maybe if my grandmother had been home he would have consulted with her, but knowing him, that might not have been likely. His word and say were always final, and he was quite forceful with his decisions. He had a very strong pride, and a lot of people attributed that to his being a self-made man who, with a minimal education, rose to the position of a cabinet secretary. It is very telling in the way I called my grandfather "Papa," which in India is a word strictly reserved for your father, and my grandmother, "Granny," like who she was for me. My grandfather did not trust anyone other than himself to keep me safe or well. He took his role as my rescuer seriously, and on most days, with suffocating consequences. Always bringing up his age and how he had only a few years to live, he wanted to be sure I was cooked, baked, and ready to come out of life's oven early and equipped to face the world. With him, it was always a race against time to make sure I was grown and educated enough to stand on my two feet if a husband could not be found for me.

My grandmother at home was the one who made sure food was made by the help. And if I needed anything sewed, she would take care of it with the skills she had developed raising seven children. Very seldom though would she have an opinion or suggestion of what was to be cooked that day. Even the daily ritual of my grandfather going to the market early in the morning to buy fresh vegetables, fish, or meat for the day's food would be undertaken without any input from my grandmother.

This way of living was what I grew up with, and never questioned. My grandfather was the only male role model I had, and in my impressionable mind, I accepted his behavior as normal. On the days he punished me or beat me, I would go crying to my grandmother, but there was not much she could do. She clearly knew where she stood and where her lines were drawn.

We had a beach house in Puri on the Bay of Bengal, about a four-hour drive from our home in Cuttack. I loved it there. It was right on the beach, and my days and afternoons would be spent gathering seashells and fir cones in my wicker basket. I loved the feel of the soft sand under my feet and between my toes. Best of all, I loved sitting on the beach looking out at the wide expanse of the sea and wondering what was on the other side of the horizon where I could see the waves rising and crashing. My love for the sea continues till this day. I feel an uncanny connection. Maybe the rolling waves had an answer to who I was or why I was. Each time they hit the shore and went back, I felt my questions go back, and with an incoming wave, I looked for my answers. Nothing came.

My grandmother loved going to Puri, too. They had, a long time ago, befriended an English lady by the name of Phyllis Watts who ran a bed and breakfast there called The Lodge. I think when my grandmother was around her, she did not feel strange or out of place.

One summer, my grandfather was getting ready to get the home whitewashed on the inside, and the outside of the home painted. This was a laborious seven-to-ten-day process, which needed supervision of the contracted labor. When my grandmother told my grandfather that she was taking me to Puri, as I had just finished my exams and needed a break, a bitter fight broke out between them. I had never seen her so strong and resolved.

My grandfather asked my grandmother to leave and go stay with one of her sons if she could not listen to him. My grandmother, needless to say, did not go to Puri. I am not sure how old I was then, but I remember after that, my grandmother kind of receded into herself and very rarely gave suggestions or input about anything that concerned me. She would go visit one of her children for a few days or weeks, but would never take me with her.

# 6

# *Between Hope and Despair*

❪ ❫

As I GREW OLDER, my resentment and anger towards my grandfather began to build up. I was afraid of him. Afraid of his temper and his beatings. Yet, I loved him, because he was the only father I knew and there were a lot of times when he would cross oceans to give me something that I wanted.

This yo-yo existence that I lived, between being loved and being punished for the littlest of things, was my undoing. I was beginning to get sneaky. At a very young age, I realized sometimes you don't have to tell the truth if you want something. Some days after school, I walked home with friends and dropped into their homes out of curiosity to see how they lived or what they did there. This was absolutely not allowed. When I was a few minutes late coming back from school, it was so easy to say we had after-school practice for a concert or sports day. Lies seemed to come easy. Sharing emotions or thoughts was more difficult.

*A studio portrait.*

Most Indians raise their children with an authoritarian style of parenting, making children follow the rules with no questions asked, and sometimes, or most times, even speaking or answering for them. Ask an Indian child what he or she wants to be or what they want to study, and out speaketh Daddy or Mommy about how they plan on being a doctor, engineer, or lawyer.

With centuries of authoritative cycles going around our culture, it is very difficult to break out of that mold. The adage "history repeats itself" is not to be taken lightly. For a while, I carried that mantle with me as I raised my son. It was hard to break that pattern of "you know what is best for your kids." Thankfully, with the world opening up and a global economy at play, parents these days are much more evolved and smarter about the decisions and repercussions their words and works might have on a child.

For someone like me, who grew up in an authoritarian home, there was no escape. This stifling, suffocating love always left me feeling like a victim. I grew resentful and angry. This, even at that early age, manifested itself in tantrums, anger bouts, lying about most things, and always being ready to give up and run. I would constantly feel slighted and hurt. Anger on most days gave way to tears: tears of anger, tears of frustration, and worst of all, tears of not being loved and wanted. I remember feeling left out and always feeling like it was me against them. The "them" being my grandparents, my aunts, my uncles, my cousins, anyone who was family, and anyone who had anything to do with the family.

On most days, I loved my cousins, and loved when they came on vacations. I grew up in a household that had three uncles and three aunts, my mother's entire siblings, and between them, twenty-one kids. This was what we Americans would call the homestead; I grew up in a home that could house more than twenty people at a time. But I was alone in it.

I looked forward to the holidays. That was when my cousins would descend from exotic parts of India. I would wait impatiently to look at their clothes, which were at least ten seasons ahead of mine. I would get a set of new clothes from someone, and best of all, I would get to eat things that I never would in the normal course of a day. I would wait to hear their stories of strolling down main streets and stopping at coffee shops, which I knew would never happen to me in a million years.

On some days I was envious and jealous of my cousins. Envious that they had someone that they could call Mumma. Envious that when they needed something, they could go running to their parents. Jealous that they had this sense of entitlement that came so naturally. If they wanted to buy something from the market or at a fair, they could ask for the money without being told, like I was, that raising me was a big expense and drain and that there was no extra money for fairs or toys.

We would spend hours together (of course only after finishing our homework)—playing dumb charades, and hide-and-go-seek. We were creative, too. Staging fashion shows, heck, once even staging a play based on Hindu Mythology in a strict Christian household headed by a Pentecost Grandfather and an Assyrian Christian Grandmother who belonged to the Orthodox Russian Church. It was a coup in those days.

*Memories with my cousins. I am the bald one.*

When each set of cousins came to visit, I would always pretend I was one of their siblings. The few times that I went out with my cousins and their parents to a stranger or a colleague's home, I was always passed off as their sister. This seemed to work very well, and I was protected from the world that was outside our immediate family and close friends. No one asked questions and no one said anything.

But we also fought. During the fights, everyone would go back to their own territory (brothers and sisters together). At the end of the day, they were siblings, and I would be the Lone Ranger. I hated taking sides. I loved them all equally. I wanted the fights over, because I was missing out on my playtime with them. They would soon be gone and I would be alone again. I would walk around the house devastated and sad for days. I would walk through their rooms, trying to see if there were any remnants of their visit left behind.

After the cousins left, our household would go back to being a silent zone, with hardly any words, discussions, or playtime involved. There was not much a child had to say to her grandparents. And other than trying to raise me to the best of their ability, there was not much two seventy year olds had to tell a seven year old.

*SILENCE*

I am awake
Awake with my thoughts
Awake with the hope that someone will knock

I sit and listen to the sounds of silence
Praying to the Gods for some kind of defiance

There will be no one I tell myself
Promises are not meant to be kept

Learn to live for yourself
Is what I tell my deluded self?

# 7

# *Cuttack*

《 》

T SEEMS MY DESTINY WAS ALWAYS CUTTACK. Close to the Bay of Bengal, Cuttack was a delta surrounded by three rivers. The town, like the sleepy rivers, was laid back, slow, and not really going anywhere. When the monsoons came, they overflowed, and when the summer came, they seemed to sink and dry.

*My parents' wedding picture.*

My parents had married in August of 1956 in Cuttack in my grandparent's home. My grandfather was not present at the wedding. He had refused to participate because my father was not a Christian, and he did not think people of different religions would be able to live together with such a great divide between them. Marry they did, and my brother, Pintu, was born in September of 1957. After they got married, they moved to different cities in India due to my father's work.

My grandfather writes:

> *Long before you were born there were some disagree-ments between your mother and father. Several such instances were however made up, but the one that arose a few months before your birth was of a serious nature and continued till long after your birth. Your mother had come away to Cuttack with your brother. After your birth your mother took up a teacher's post in a local school and began to neglect you and your brother.*

As I follow my life's trajectory in those few short years of three, I can see how unstable my life was. One day, I am in Cuttack, the next in Delhi, back again to Cuttack, some-times with my brother, sometimes without, sometimes with my parents, and sometimes without. Maybe that explains the restlessness I still have within me. The restlessness of want-ing to be someone else or live like someone else was always a driving force within me. I always felt lacking and inadequate. Everyone else that I knew seemed to live such a different life than mine. They had siblings they shared life with, they had vacations that they took with their families, and most of all, they had stories to share. They had roots; they had connections to so many different offshoots of their family. One summer they spent with their father's parents, one summer they spent with their mother's parents, and every story boasted of family bonding and fun. I had no such stories to tell. Growing up, I always felt like I lived in the shadows. Dark, long shadows full of secrets hovered over me.

Growing up in 1960s India and living in a small town where everyone knew each other, not many questions were asked inside our home. If you didn't ask, the problems did not exist. If you did not know, then people would not know—a philosophy that has governed me throughout my life.

I digress. Let me go back to the disagreements that my grandfather talks about. Apparently, a few years before my parents filed for a divorce in 1968, my father had filed his own case for divorce. It was a few months after I was born.

*A year previous to this a divorce case was instituted by your father on the grounds, among others, that you were an illegitimate child and that he was not your father. This case did not, however, get pushed to the final conclusion.*

This fact, that my father disowned me even before I was born, was always handled with great care by my grandparents and my aunts and uncles when I got to an age where I could have asked questions. They couched it in small comfortable words. "There was no other way in those days to get a divorce unless one could prove infidelity."

This turned out to be a piece of information that I was deeply ashamed off. There were so many words that had no dignity for a child that was born illegitimately. I cringed every time I saw a Bollywood movie that invariably had a child who turned out to be the hero or heroine of the movie who did not have a noble beginning. In my mind, I started identifying with the less fortunate. The class structure in India clearly defines what position you occupy in society and I had absolutely no pride in the class of society I was born into. I was already shunned and felt differentiated by them.

*At that time, your mother was in Cuttack. But later, your father came and took you all back to Delhi. He showed much love for you, though a few months back when I was pleading with him for you, he had flatly refused to own you and said, "an illegitimate child should not be dumped on me." He wrote that if he has to take you over, I must give him money. He mentioned some thousands to run a business for his and your benefit. This I thought was sheer blackmailing. Although I have helped him financially on many occasions, I was not prepared to give him any more money which he might squander away like before. This broke my heart. I found your mother equally cold about you and was not willing to take on any responsibility for you. In the particular circumstances of your birth when your father has disowned you, it is natural that a mother should bestow upon you 100 fold loves. But you have been denied this most shockingly and though she has given birth to you she is bereft of natural feeling for you. Although you have been forsaken by your parents and deprived of their love and care, God has not forsaken you.*

I am not really sure when I became aware of the fact that my father had asked for money to raise me. Like a bribe. Or what do you call it? I never connected his statement of disowning me, calling me illegitimate, and filing for a divorce on those grounds to him asking for money to raise me. Maybe I was too young to understand the meaning of the word illegitimate. Maybe he was justified.

My father was always a mythical figure for me. I don't remember his face, his voice, or his demeanor. I don't remember any moments with him. Sometimes, very rarely, I see a face, way back in my mind. A voice that is deep and a body language that is not very welcoming. I remember a room, being a child, my brother in the room also, older, playing by my side. I hear footsteps. I hear my brother calling out to me, and then I don't hear footsteps or my brother's voice. I sense being alone in a room in a house. All by myself.

To be honest, I don't know if I am actually reliving a moment or a time from my past or basing it on what my grandmother told me.

*You were only two years old. That cruel man, he left you on the floor playing, all alone in the house, your mother had gone to work and the maid was taking a nap. He picked up your brother and left. He has a heart of nails. You could have been kidnapped. You could have fallen and hurt yourself. He did not care. He always hated you.*

A lot of my answers, maybe not answers, but a fog that finally got cleared, lay in my grandfather's diary. Writing diligently almost every day, my grandfather stuck to facts, disappointments, dirty secrets, and duty. When I was eleven, I finally figured out how to get to that book. Leave no stone unturned, isn't that what they say, when you need to get to the bottom of things? Well, that is what I did. A stone, that is all it took to break the lock on his cupboard.

> *What pains me most is that twice you removed small coins from the tin on my dressing table without my knowledge. This amounts to stealing. When you are caught—because I know how many coins I have kept—you deny. This is lying. So you steal and tell lies. You take it to school to buy sweets and some other rubbish things from the man with his cart in school. I do not want you to eat those things and spoil your stomach. I also heard that once or twice you took coins from your mother's table. I am very, very unhappy about this and often prayed to God to correct you. I also punish you sometimes with a cane. For you, I have a cane in the dining room, because sometimes you give trouble for eating. One cane is kept on the verandah where I sit and shave in the morning, because very often I have to make you sit by my side to have your early breakfast. Then there is another cane in my room next to my bed where you sit and do your homework. When you do not do your lessons properly, I have to cane you.*

This entry in my grandfather's journal I read when I must have been eleven or twelve. Or maybe earlier, I don't know. What is clear from his entry is that around that age I had started acting up. "Acting up" was not a phrase used while I was growing up; it was classified as misbehaving or being disobedient. The tougher words used were stealing and lying.

I remember picking up coins from my grandfather's dressing table to buy snacks at school like all the other kids. I knew if I asked for money, it would never be given to me. So I took it. Stole it, I guess. I just wanted to fit in. I wanted to be just like the other kids. Why did I always have to be different? Just because I did not have parents, did that mean I was poor and could not buy stuff like all the other kids? I wanted to be liked. Oh, how I wanted to be liked. And the only way to achieve that was to be one with them, shoulder to shoulder, participating and doing everything they did.

Corporal punishment seemed to be an integral part of my life. I remember going to school with welts showing on my legs. When questioned about them by my friends, my answer was ready: I fell off the guava tree.

The shame and the hurt that I felt never led me to ask my friends if they were ever caned at home. Even if they were, I had already decided in my mind that I was being caned because I never really belonged. I was an outcast, and not one of the Samuels.

Somehow, deep down inside, I had convinced myself that I deserved it. The feeling that I was worth something never really surfaced. If a mother does not think you are worth keeping or fighting for, then I guess your self-worth has already been shattered. If a father claims you are not his, then is there anything else that can keep you grounded with a sense of belonging or make you emotionally strong?

I am pretty sure that's where my journey of accepting abuse, mainly from men, started. Very early in life I developed this sense of not being good enough for anyone or anything. I did not expect anything from anyone.

*It pains me very much to cane you, but I have to punish you or else you will be spoilt. How much I love you, you can never imagine and by the time to realize it, I will have vanished from this world.*

*You returned from school, but you came with another girl of your class. When questioned you said you had come to drop your school bag at home and then go back for film show in school. You could have sent the bag back with the rickshaw man as on previous occasions. But the real fact is you wanted to have a joy ride with your friend.*

I was six years old and being a kid was not permitted. I still remember the humiliation I felt as I was being admonished with my friend standing next to me. It did not help my situation that my aunts and uncles, my mother's siblings, would constantly tell my grandfather that he was spoiling me, that he was making me greedy and needed to be strict with me, otherwise I would grow up to be loose. Were they ever there to see the punishment meted out? Did their hearts beat for me, the way they would beat for their own children? Did they know his financial circumstances? No income came in other than his pension, which never rose with inflation or the passing years, and the house rent from our downstairs floor. And so, he was raising a child in those circumstances and giving her an education, which in India is not free, and giving her what she needed or wanted in this new age of child-rearing that he had no idea of.

Amongst other trimmings of lifestyle and needs, the food in our home was rationed. However hungry I got, I could not have more than two chapattis at night, and the rice during the day was served in the amount he thought a girl of my age and his finances could handle. The same curry that we had in the morning would be eaten at night. Other than birthdays or Christmas, food was never brought from the outside.

Did they know all this when I would take an extra sausage or lunch meat that an aunt had brought from overseas and be admonished for it? Called greedy and selfish? Eating out was a luxury that my grandfather would never entertain. I remember that when one of my uncles or aunts visited, before leaving they would give my grandmother pocket money. Of course, my grandfather would never be told about this.

My grandmother and I both loved eating Chinese food. Hong Kong was a restaurant just caddy corner away from our home. Once, when my grandfather had retired to his room for the night, I ran across to the restaurant, put in my order of fried rice and chili chicken, paid them, and ran back home, hoping and praying he hadn't stepped out of his room. Thirty minutes later I ran back to pick it up. My grandmother and I sat in the drawing room and gobbled it down with one ear tuned to his footsteps.

Did my extended family not see that when we all got together, and when everyone went for midnight picnics on the river, I was the only one not allowed to go? No amount of crying, tantrums, or anger would melt my grandfather's heart. For some reason, he thought I would not be safe with anyone but him. Did they not see how my little heart was crushed, how left out I felt? But no one, not one of my five aunts and uncles, ever stood up for me. I was a bad tempered, obstinate child who talked back.

Today, all of my aunts and uncles are gone from this world. I bear no grudges against them, but I so wish I'd had the courage when they were alive to tell them, ask them, why they could not have stood up for me a little more. They had all left their hometown of Cuttack in search of better opportunities for themselves and their children, but not one of them stopped to look back and see that there was another child being left behind, emotionally, physically, and mentally.

I still remember how fascinated I used to be when the extended family visited, especially the ones that lived overseas. Their suitcases, clothes, shoes, the goodies inside their bags all looked and smelt different. If I close my eyes now, I can still get the scent of a "foreign smell."

Not having seen anything like this, I admit I took some things that I should not have. I remember taking and hiding a desk clock that one of my aunts had brought. Of course, even though I did not admit to it, I was called a thief and a kleptomaniac. Really, a kleptomaniac at eight, when I did not even know the meaning of the word? Needless to say, one of the three canes that my grandfather had for me was used that evening. That aunt never forgave me, ever. And there was not one occasion that she did not show her displeasure or dislike for me. She would tell her father that he was wasting his time and money on me. In her opinion, I was running wild and needed to be reeled in.

I will not forget that when it was gift-giving time, my gift would always be some kind of hand-me-down. The first time I asked for anything was a tape player when I was a teenager. It was like I had asked for the Kohinoor diamond. I never heard the end of that.

I always believed that my grandfather's children were protective of their father. They felt that as their father, he had done enough. He had raised seven children and now it was his time to relax and unwind. My being there was an intrusion into their lives. I was never allowed to forget that grateful was what I should have been every waking moment. Burdened with that thought, life growing up was always about being less of a person, an interloper, and a person who did not deserve a life from the sacrifices two old people were making. So being a kid, and whatever else came with it, was essentially something that I should not or could not be doing.

Growing up for me was a lot of work. Some days more than others, it would get to me. I remember running away from home so many times. I don't think I was more than four or five. What that meant at that age was disappearing for a while, sitting on a tree or lying on the tin roof tops of one of our outhouses while gazing at the stars and moon and wondering what and where my life was going to take me and always longing for something that I never had. I wanted so badly to be loved, to be accepted, and to not be left with the feeling of being an outsider.

# 8

# *And Then She was Gone*

❨ ❩

MY MOTHER CAME BACK TO CUTTACK when I was five. The reason I say that with such certainty is because my mother left home again when I was seven. In my life, I have a lot of Before My Mother Left moments, and After My Mother Left moments. That is how I keep track of my history and weave my story together.

After my mother returned, there was a lot of turmoil within the family. My grandparents were constantly angry. My mother was constantly gone. When she was home, she was to me this mysterious woman, always perfectly dressed, always perfectly accessorized, and always perfectly coiffured. She was either in her room reading, correcting school home-work for the kids at the school she worked at, or just being reclusive and uncommunicative. Never once do I remember her asking me what I was doing, what I had eaten, whether I had done my homework, or even being a mother, just picking me up or giving me a hug. I don't remember having any kind of conversations with her. She was aloof to the point of not caring. Maybe she was thinking about my brother. Maybe that is why she never hugged me or kissed me. Maybe she thought my brother would be sad if she loved me and didn't get to love him.

This is how I consoled myself.

My mother was a beautiful woman and from what I was told later, had won many a local beauty contest. She was always elegantly dressed. Never did I seen her in sloppy clothes or sloppy gait. Her room, which was out of bounds for me when she was at home, beckoned me. I snuck in when she was not there to look at her shoes and try them on, to look at the bottles of perfume on her dressing table and sniff each one, to look at the lipsticks and the nail polishes and then go into her cupboard to drape her saris around me. I would always make sure not to move her things around. I knew I would be in trouble if I did.

I was young, but my mind was beginning to see things, to distinguish between the feelings of being wanted and not wanted. In conversation, when my aunts and uncles would come to visit, there was always a talk or discussion about what my mother was doing with her life. I would listen behind doors. I would get angry behind doors, and I would cry behind doors. Even with all these emotions, I don't think I ever had the feeling that I needed to defend her or protect her.

I remember a suitor coming to meet her. He was a family

friend's son and therefore was allowed to stay in our home. I remember him driving up in an open-air jeep, the likes of which I had never seen in my life. He brought me chocolates, said hello to me, and once asked me if I wanted a ride. I ran to my room, got ready, pulled on my gumboots, because that is what people wore when they rode in jeeps, and was ready to go. Growing up, we never had a car, and I don't think I had sat in many. So that was another attraction for me: I could ride about town and show my schoolmates how cool I was.

I remember my mother saying no, that I was too young to be sitting in one. I was crestfallen and heartbroken. I remember going back to my room and standing by the window and crying my heart out. I guess she did not want to be saddled with a child or responsibility. Maybe she was trying to tell Mr. Suitor that she would be entering this relationship with him alone, with no baggage.

My dreams of leaving my hometown never went anywhere. Mr. Suitor left after a few days, and I never saw him again. Then again, for a few months, every evening I would see her go out. Mr. Suitor Number Two never came inside the house, so I never really knew him. I often stood at my bedroom window and stuck my tongue out at him. Some days she would come back from dates with flowers, and some days she would come back with chocolates. I would wait for the chocolates. But sharing was something she never did. I remember her sitting one after- noon on our verandah and correcting her school homework for the kids. The chocolates sat on the ledge by her side. I kept walking up and down our long verandah, hoping she would see me, hoping that if I made my presence felt, she would give me a chocolate. Nothing happened. She did not look up at me or acknowledge my presence.

I went back into my room and waited. Waited like a predator in the jungle, who silently watches behind a tree or a bush for the best time to jump on its prey. I was that predator. I knew at some point she would get up and leave the chocolate unguarded. Well, she did. As soon as she walked away, I darted in to the verandah and picked up the candy bar and ran back to my room. In the pile that she had there, I was sure that she would not miss one. Miss it she did. "Did you take a chocolate? Don't touch those chocolates, they are mine."

I don't think I said anything to her other than denying that I took them. She reported me to my grandfather, because this was the second time I had stolen her candy. My grandfather did the only thing he could do when he thought I was not behaving well. Out came the cane: One swat for stealing, one swat for lying, and one swat for being shameless. The rest of the day I spent in my room, crying myself to sleep and wondering at why I always got caned, and why I was always doing something wrong. Is it any surprise that as an adult, when I went into get an allergy test done to find out the root cause of my debilitating migraines, chocolate was the trigger?

*Last night you expressed a desire to sleep with your mother at night. Since childhood you had not slept with her except when you were a few months old. I was anxious because in this winter cold your mother keeps all the windows and doors open in her room. I only wish your mother*

*did take real mother's interest in you, so that my burden for*
*you will become less and I will be happy for you. But this*
*is not to be. Your mother cannot sacrifice her pleasure and*
*comforts for you.*

*You can never know what I am sacrificing for you—*
*money, labor, time and everything which will give me rest*
*and peace at this old age.*

It was then maybe that I started thinking that I needed to
be less of a burden—that I needed to find a home for myself
where I would not be a liability. I remember many a time
loading up my bicycle with a few of my belongings and just
riding the streets in the afternoons when my grandparents
were asleep.

My first thought was to go look for my brothers and sisters, though I did not know whom my family consisted of.
Every day, in my mind, I had an addition or a subtraction
to my family, all depending on our interactions in my mind.
Needless to say, someone known on the streets would see
me and report back to my grandfather. Out came the cane.
Out came the words "ungrateful," "wretched," and "wicked
child."

A few months, or maybe it was a few weeks after that, the
silence in our home was ripped with fights, tears, admonish-
ments, and a lot of yelling. My mother had decided to marry
the person who came every day to pick her up and take her
out. From what I sensed and heard, my grandparents were
trying to tell her it was not the right thing to do—that she
had a child, that she had a home, that she had parents to
support her, that she should not throw everything away. This
went on for days.

I remember peeping into her room and seeing her pack her things a little bit at a time. I went to our storage unit and pulled out a suitcase and hid it under my bed, hoping that she would walk in and say, "Pack your bags, we are leaving." Days went by, still nothing.

To draw attention to myself, I snuck into her room again, which was the last time I ever would. I opened her cupboard. I guess I was trying to see what was left in there. To my bad luck, she walked back into her room smacked my hand and called out to my grandfather.

He walked into the room and stood at a distance, listening quietly to her. "You are going to lose another child," he said.

Even at that age, I knew he was talking about my brother. I knew he sometimes looked at my brother's pictures in his album, and I knew he sometimes referred to my brother in conversations with my grandmother when he thought I was not listening. I was always listening. Listening to voices, to commands, to anything that had a sound, because sometimes the quietness around me irked me.

In my child's mind, I knew something had shifted that day. My grandfather did not hit me or cane me. He was always so particular about the way I behaved, always so particular that I did the right thing, and always so willing to take his anger about someone else out on me. That day it was different. It was like he had no energy left. Or maybe, he knew what was going to happen. It was as if he wanted to protect me from time, protect me from the future, and protect me from everything that would hurt at that moment. No one really thinks that a child needs protection from her own mother.

One sunny afternoon atop the terrace leading to the steps of the house, I saw my mother with a suitcase in her hand. Wrapped in a flowing chiffon sari with a *bindi* on her forehead, she walked out without looking back, a leather-buckled suitcase in her hand. My grandmother trailed behind her, crying. My grandfather stood at the foot of the stairs.

"If you walk out without this child, you will never see her again," he said.

I ran down the terrace and wrapped both of my arms around her knees. Without tears or even so much as a sound, she disentangled herself from me.

# 9

# *My Most Honored Guests Were the Ones who Never Came*

❪ ❫

As a child in India, the day before my birthday (March 31) was always a day filled with excitement. It was the day the tailor brought home my new clothes, the day the baker brought home my cake, and the day the household help went shopping for the tea party that was to be held in my honor on the first of April. I would sit on the porch steps and wonder who would give me what as a present. Would Mrs. Tucker give me the fourth book of the Famous Five by Enid Blyton? How much money might Aunty Radha put in my birthday card? Why did Papa and Granny insist on giving clothes as presents?

But another thought persisted above all the others: maybe, just maybe, the joke would finally be over. My parents would come to my party as a surprise, scoop me up in their arms, and wish me a happy birthday.

Maybe I could finally go to school and not have my friends ask questions about Papa and Granny that filled me with embarrassment and shame: "Why is your father so old?," or "How come your mother wears a dress and has blue eyes?"

The embarrassment and shame I experienced as a child over the absence of my parents made me a person who spun exceptional tales about my life, stories that would have put Stephen King or John Grisham to shame. "My parents?" I would say, "They are spies for the Indian Army and live abroad, most likely London."

When extended family came to stay, on most days you would find me sitting behind a curtain or perched precariously on a balcony, sometimes even hiding under the bed, listening. Eavesdropping to glean information from conversations was how I related to my family. I tried to piece together my history from the hushed-tone phrases I could string together: poor child . . . orphanage . . . what a trauma . . . how could a mother do such a thing?

I knew better than to ask—no one would explain anything to me. It seemed my grandparents' plan was that the words mother, father, mummy, or daddy were never to be mentioned in front of me.

Still, I persisted with my hope of a birthday surprise. I wanted my parents—the young, age-appropriate ones. I wanted a normal dad who would drive a car and take me to school. A mother who was beautiful and ethereal in a sari, who would drop everything she was doing and hug me when I came back from school. I knew other, younger parents did this. I had seen my friends. I carried around a lot of envy and sadness.

But maybe, just maybe, this was the year.

The first of April came, the only day I was allowed to sleep late. Schools were closed because it was a government holiday: Orissa Day, a celebration to mark the state as a separate province. I wasn't able to give out toffees to my classmates, as I would have been allowed to if my birthday fell on a school day. On my birthday, there was no special breakfast and no phone calls from relatives—mostly because we didn't have a phone.

All of my focus fell to the grandfather clock in the dining room, waiting for the clock to strike 4:00 PM. As the cucumber finger sandwiches were being made and the meat patties were warmed, I excitedly put on my new clothes. My favorites were a forty-inch-wide bell bottom set (I was a real trendsetter in those days). And then I waited for friends to show up.

The ones who came, though, were mostly family friends, hardly anyone in my age group. One by one, they wished me a happy birthday and handed over their wrapped presents. In my mind, I sized up the package while speculating on the gift. *Darn, that's a box of chocolates. Why? Couldn't she give me like a book or a dress or something?* This went on for a little while. In between silly talk and little foods, I would sneak back and forth into my room and open the presents one by one. Always glimpsing out of the window, always with ears perked for new voices, I kept hoping and dreaming. But they never came.

Slowly, year after year, the same old routine became boring. Of course, once I hit twelve, the party was over. "Too old to have a birthday party," my grandparents would say. The clothes, the sandwiches, the meat patties, the cake—all gone. What never went away was the longing, the hope, and the sadness that "they" never came.

Here I am, forty years later, feeling nostalgic for those days of excitement—the moments of being carefree, the future of endless possibilities, the anticipation, the innocence, and the dreams.

The one flame that has never died and carries with it a ray of hope: they will come and they will say they are sorry we left you and went away—and they will, at last, finally, wish me a happy birthday.

# 10

# *Faces*

❨ ❩

**M**Y RANDFATHER WAS AFRAID that after he passed away, my parents, who were in the eyes of the law my legal guardians, would claim ownership of me to get their hands on the money or any property my grandfather would leave behind for me.

> *I wanted to completely remove you from the control of your mother, who according to the law is your legal guardian. Although for all practical purposes, she has been dead to you for the last seven years, yet the law will give her the rights to claim you if she wants. I thought that after my death she will exercise her claim to lay her hands on the money I shall leave for your future on the grounds of you being a minor and she being your legal guardian. So I asked my lawyer to institute a case in the court of law to*

*declare her as an unfit mother. However before taking recourse to the law courts my lawyer asked your mother whether she would willingly hand over your guardianship to me. To which your mother readily consented.*

This relinquishment happened on December 31, 1968. I take that back. The formal official relinquishment happened on that day. The unofficial relinquishment happened the day I was born, April 1, 1961. It took her all of seven years to finally get rid of me.

My mother had left a few months before the relinquishment. Maybe it was the summer of 1968. I do not remember the time, the month or the date, but I do remember the day. My grandfather, who documented every single milestone in my life, did not write anything about that day.

My mother's letter to the lawyer reads:

*Dear Mr. Murthy,*

*Received your note. I have already written to Delhi but it would be nice if you could pen a few lines of course. I have given your reference.*

*You can arrange for finalization any day (of the adoption) preferably during the morning hours.*

*Yours sincerely*

Here was a woman, a mother, who wrote about the adoption or referred to the adoption as something that was normal, that it was something people did every day and also something that was inconvenient for her. In the letter, she gives the lawyer a time "preferably during the morning hours." I keep re-reading that letter and keep wondering what in her day was so important that coming to sign the papers needed to fit in with her schedule.

After my mother left, I remember spending my afternoons or mornings when I was not in school walking through a banana grove that my grandfather had started in our garden. He had lined up the trees in straight lines of three. There must have been at least seven rows. I would pretend these trees were human beings and have long, drawn-out conversations with then. My other refuge was the guava tree, where I spent long hours perched on the highest branch, reading a comic book and eating guavas. The outdoors, the grass, the birds, and the breeze was where I would always be. I did not like staying indoors. Her room was empty, and I still smelt the lacto=calamine lotion she used in the evenings to keep mosquitoes away. Till this day, I cannot use that lotion. It nauseates me.

After her departure, I knew my grandfather began writing to boarding schools all over the country. He wanted me to have the best education possible, he said. The small town we lived in might not have the best possibilities, he said. I would hear him from my room, typing away all afternoon on his desk with the typewriter when everyone else was down for a siesta. There was no siesta for me. My ears would be tuned to his room, the rustling of the white sheet of papers, the carbon between the papers, and his typewriter knob turning while he lined up the two sheets with the carbon in-between, feeding it into the machine. Clack,

clack, the typewriter would go, his fingers tapping away at the keys, spilling out his words.

*Dear Rev Welsh,*

*I write to you to ask for compassion in admitting my ward, Shabnam Singh, to your school. Having being born into peculiar and unprecedented circumstances . . .*

With each turning of the typewriter knob, I knew exactly how many letters he had typed. I did not know which boarding school or how far away I was going. Nobody talked; nothing was discussed. I would wait patiently till the grandfather clock in our dining room struck 4:00. I knew that was when, after his cup of tea, he would head out to the post office to mail the letters. His leaving the house was when I found out about my life. I would sneak into his room and go look at the file on his table, which I knew was where all the letters, all neatly filed in a three-ringed file, would be. Darjeeling, Shimla, Koidaikanal, Ranchi—these were names of cities and places far, far away from where I lived.

Why was he sending me away? Did he not know that I was frightened? Frightened to leave the house, to be with other kids, to talk to older people. What if I went somewhere and came back and there was nobody here? Where would I go, who would I live with, what would I do?

I hated being inside the house. I never studied, I never listened, and I hardly ever did what I was told, unless there was a cane staring at me. I would backchat and be rebellious. When I was finally accepted by a school that met all my grandfather's expectations, I started to feel slightly excited. It would be a new experience for me. I would have people to talk to, play with, and eat with. Study was never foremost on my mind. The process of shopping for my uniforms, shoes, books, and other sundries that I needed off the list that the school had sent made me feel special. I don't think I had ever been the center of so much focus. I think, for the first time, I felt that I was important.

When the time came to leave Cuttack with my trunk and my tuck box packed, the reality of leaving everything familiar tugged at me. My grandparents were the only two people who I really knew in this world, and now I was going away to a land that was new and people who were new. I wondered if they would be able to tell that I was different.

I wondered that if they could tell that just a few months before I was getting ready to leave for school, our tenant's household help had pulled me to a side of the house that no one frequented and touched me in places to see if I had become a "big girl." I had no idea what he meant. All I felt were his rough hands on me and the smell on his body. That smell has still not left my nose. That smell I sniff and try to smell on any man that I come across. That smell tells me danger lurks.

My grandmother had told me ever since I could remember: "Remember, men are bad."

"They will tell you bad things, they will do bad things."

"Don't be alone with them."

Despite these warnings, I went when he told me that he wanted to see if I was a big girl. I knew if I told my grandmother, she would beat me or tell my grandfather, who might cane me for being bad. I came back to my room and wondered what he was checking for. It bothered me, but I did not know what to do or what to say.

I wondered if the girls in the boarding school would smell this man on me and would be able to tell that I was bad.

I cannot remember how old I was. Six, seven, eleven, thirteen? How does one keep track of the time when one is so young? Does time mean anything at that age? But how does one not remember at what age one was molested or raped? I might have been only eight years old, but I still remember what he said to me, where he took me, and what he did to me. I still remember who he was, and I still know who he is.

I remember all their faces. There were four different people. Different ones at the different ages I was. I know their names. I see their faces when I close my eyes. The horror, the guilt, the shame, the nightmares, and the feeling that I was no good have stayed with me from eight to fifty-five. Was I molested, or was I raped? Is there a difference? How does one know? Who does one ask? At eight, one does not even know what was done. I have never told anyone. This is the first time I am writing about it, talking about it, and giving those dark days a shape and a form. I held on to this secret through an engagement, a marriage, and a child. I held on to this secret for fifty years.

⊄ ⊅

I left for school. Located behind high walls, the boarding school felt like a fortress where an evil king lived, the sort of dark ruler I knew from books. Some days I had fun in school, but on most days I felt out of place, withdrawn, and sad. The girls had so many stories to share, some happy, some angry, and some sad. I did not know what I could share. I had a habit of stuffing words and feelings inside of me. I never felt like I was part of life. I always seemed to be looking in from the outside.

Once school started, I volunteered for chores. The older girls in the dorm would make you a part of their inner circle if you washed their socks or cleaned their shoes. I needed to do that. I needed to be a part of something that made me feel accepted.

On my first school break from boarding school, I came home to new tenants in the house. The downstairs had been rented out to a local insurance company. In the afternoons, I would roam the gardens while my grandparents napped. On one such summer afternoon, when the doors and windows were shut to keep out the heat, one of the people who worked at the office, who I called uncle because he was older than me and that's what Indians do out of respect for age, called me into the office to chat. I loved going into the office because it made me feel all grown up. He pinched my lips with his fingers and said, "You are so pretty." I smiled, feeling good.

"Come here"

I went. He held me against him, facing him. I knew what he was doing was something that he was not supposed to do. This uncle was married; this uncle had a daughter. This uncle, his wife and his daughter used to come over for tea and snacks and would sit for hours talking to my grandparents without him even batting an eyelid. I was told for many afternoons I was pretty.

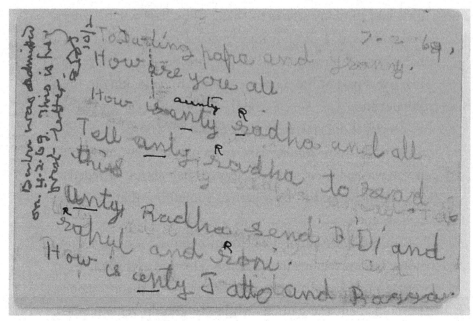

*A letter from my boarding school.*

I went back to boarding school carrying some more haunting moments with me. Why I never had the courage to walk away or say anything is beyond my understanding.

At eleven, when I came back from boarding school for good, I was a little more rebellious and a little more disobedient. Despite being told I was a girl and needed to be calmer and ladylike, I still climbed trees, flew kites, played marbles with the boys, and played cricket, which at that time was only a man's sport.

One day, while I was gathering up my belongings to walk upstairs, the peon (assistant) who worked in the office followed me up the stairs, the dark dingy steps that led from our backyard downstairs to our kitchen terrace upstairs. These were the same steps that my mother had used when she walked out of the house with her suitcase in her hand.

Those steps had some kind of power over me. Just before I reached the landing, he pulled me back, turned me around, and hurt me like I was never hurt before. Blood trickled down my legs, and I did not know why. His body odor stunk. If I sniff real hard even now, I feel it permeate through me and it makes me sick to the pit of my stomach. I could not tell anyone anything. My grandparents were certainly not people I could go to with what had just happened.

Within a year or so at school, I started to question the authorities and give away my belongings to boarding mates. It made me feel like I was powerful, and it made the girls like me more. My grades were falling rapidly. I was always in the infirmary with some illness or another, both imaginary and real. I had stopped writing my once-a-week postcard home. Not getting good reports from the school and from my local guardian, who complained that every time I came to visit on the weekends I came with a bunch of girls, my grandfather after three years thought I was wasting his money and I was taken out of school and brought back to Cuttack. I felt victorious. I had survived being abandoned.

The house, our home, was where I wanted to be. I did not know it then, but know it now, that panic attacks were what I used to get every time that I left home. I wanted to go out of the house, but I feared that if I left and came back, something or someone would be gone.

# 11

# *My Name*

❨ ❩

ALMOST FOUR YEARS AFTER MY MOTHER LEFT, I saw her while walking to school. I saw her in a rickshaw, riding to the school she taught at, with two other children who appeared to be considerably younger than me.

There was no acknowledgement from her: no waving, no stopping to ask how I was doing without her. Life continued. From my vantage point in the crossroads of our tiny town, the life I could have shared with a mother and siblings unfolded every morning at 8:00 A.M. This continued until I left high school and went to college. Our paths never took the same roads again.

For almost seven years, I saw the little girl and the little boy go from being little babies to almost adults. I knew they had to be my siblings, my half-siblings, maybe, but still. I knew them, because I knew their mother. They didn't know me, because they did not know their mother was anything else but their mother.

A lot of evenings I would see the four of them come for dinner to the Chinese restaurant that was three doors down from our home. In a rickshaw, the girl on her father's lap, and the boy, who was younger, on his mother's lap. They looked so complete. I would sit on the windowsill in our drawing room with the lights turned off, watching them get off the rickshaw and go inside. I would sit there till they came out an hour or so later.

I knew that my mother and her own siblings were in touch. They would go see her, because she was not allowed to come to my grandparent's home. And once they came back after visiting with her, there would be no talks about her or her family in the home.

In my early teens, one of my uncles was getting ready to migrate to Australia. Before he left the country, he came home with his family to spend a month with my grandparents. It was then that he gave my grandfather an ultimatum. He wanted his sister and her family to start coming home. Under duress, my grandfather agreed, but every time my mother and her family visited, he would take me to his room, lock the door, and keep me there with him. He did not want me to see them or interact with them.

Later on in life, I realized that even though my half-siblings came home, to the very home that I was living and breathing in, they had no idea that they had an older sister. My name was never brought up, and nothing about me was ever said.

Each of my aunts and uncles played a part. I am surprised that none of them thought it was not right for people to pretend that I did not exist. They had children themselves. How would they have felt?

*The official name-change announcement in the local newspaper.*

This identity is what I struggle with every day of my life. I struggle with my name. I struggle with my last name. I struggle with the last name that I was born with, and the last name that I was adopted with. When I was nine years old, on January 19, 1970, my grandparents legally adopted me and changed my last name from Singh (which was my father's last name) to Samuel (which was my grandfather's last name). I remember my grandfather having four extra newspapers delivered that day. In those days, and I think it is still true today, any changes to a person, be it with name, marriage, divorce, or business setups, get published in newspapers. It is a proclamation to the world. To make sure no one missed the event.

As a child, that was not easy for me. Everyone and their cousin in that town that I lived in had this newspaper delivered to their homes. The night it was published, the newspapers were delivered after 8 P.M.; I sat up waiting for the newspaper boy to fling the paper inside our verandah. I don't remember being asked if I was okay with having my name changed. In fact I don't even remember being told that my name was going to be changed. As usual, my eavesdropping told me what was going on.

I remember going through all my school books, my bible, my storybooks, anything that had the name Singh on it, and running a pen through my last name and writing "Samuel." With this change of my last name, I felt a peeling away of my skin, my heart, my mind, and my emotions. At that age, I had still not comprehended what this meant in its truest form. All I knew and felt was that someone did not want me, someone did not care for me, and someone just wanted to be rid of me. This identity that I had created in my head about who I was, this little Punjabi (the region in India where my father was from) girl, who had long hair and wore her hair in two plaits like all good Punjabi girls did, who loved the food that came from that region, the raw onions that I loved eating, like most Punjabis did, the little silver kadha that I wore, all representative of my culture and faith. These were all being stripped from me. I had no identity, no culture, and no faith to proclaim as my own.

Growing up, I wanted names like Nandini, Vandana, and Geetanjali. Each name, like most Indian names, has Indian mythological roots and a different story behind it. Each name tells the world of your heritage and the region you come from. I never did want the name Shabnam. It did not allow me to blend in—blend in with the majority of my friends who had "typical" Indian first names and last.

In a country like India, where a name can tell your state, religion, what kind of food you eat, and what kind of clothes you wear, my name was a misnomer. Shabnam Samuel: Shabnam, meaning dew drops in Persian, is a common name for people of the Muslim faith. So automatically, I was asked if I was Muslim, but then Samuel: Are you a Christian?

My grandfather was a six-foot-tall Indian ,who fought in the two world wars and wore business suits and a top hat almost every day (his legacy from the British who ruled India when he was growing up), was almost like an outsider in his own little sleepy town. My grandmother, who was short and stocky, had blue eyes, wore a dress, covered her head with a scarf, and called herself an Orthodox Russian from Tbilisi, USSR, did not help my cause.

Kids in school would always wonder at my heritage, where the few blue eyes you saw were in school with teachers like Ms. James, Mr. Saunders, and Mr. Hampshire, to name a few. I grew up all day long with blue eyes.

I still don't know why I was named Shabnam. Again, it was one of those things that you were not allowed to discuss or question. And I did not have a name for a year and a half after I was born. It seems my brother, who was four when I was born, christened me Bubu when I was born, and that has remained my nickname. Again with everything else that remains unusual and peculiar in my life, it seems no one had the time, the inclination, or the need to find me a name or give me a name. Once again, was I not important enough? Was being a girl so bad, or was my ownership so disputed that they did not find a state or a person or a culture to identify me with, to give me a name that would hint at my origins?

*Your father came to Cuttack on the 26th of October, 1962. He brought some new clothes for you and I was happy to see him carrying you about in his lap. I thought that his apathetic feeling about you had changed, but I was wrong in my belief as was proved later. While here, we asked your father to give your name, which he did by naming you SHABNAM.*

And with all the confusion and secrets that corrode into my life, the irony is that the man who named me was the same man who disowned me when I was born, saying I was illegitimate. I speculate and think a lot about this. Did he name me Shabnam because he knew who my father was? Or did he name me so because he loved writing ghazals (Urdu poetry), and Shabnam was used quite often in poems? I cannot ask him and so I will never know.

I have always wondered about why my name is so different, why it had no identity of its own. There were no identifying cultural, religious, or language marks that linked my name to my circumstances, to my parents, who I was supposed to have been born to, and to the states that I came from, Delhi/Punjab in the north where my father hailed from, or Orissa on the east of India where my mother hailed from.

This sense of alienation, this sense of not belonging, set into my life very early. When you feel rootless, when you don't know the ground you sprang from, things in your life begin to look different. Does that mean I am different? Yes, on reflection, everything about me became different. I was always searching for an identity, a name, a family to claim and belong to, a sense of history to be a part of. There was nothing for me to peg my identity on. The seeds of an identity crisis were being sowed.

I do not know if it was a conscious decision, or if somewhere down in my subconscious, but I decided to become different. When I was sent to boarding school in the 3rd grade, there I was with Janet and Kathleen, and I became Jenny Samuel, Jen Samuel, if you please. Markers inserted my middle name on everything: my locker, my tuck box, my trunk, and my books. Yes, my parents were in England and I was sent here to study. My clothes and shoes spoke for themselves. For three years, I played the part of Jen.

There are days when I wish I had remained a Jen. With Jen, I found my identity. I did not have to explain my heritage. Never have I found more comfort than in the name Jen. I no longer had to hide the fact that my parents were different. Yes, I could be a Christian, and yes, I could be not all Indian.

Then three years later, it was back to my little town. My old school was the same except there were no Janets or Kathleens. Shabnam was back. The milieu was different. What a drastic change in personalities. A dew drop, who sits on a flower or a blade of grass, never saying much, but swaying in the breeze and hanging on for dear life. Watch a dew drop next time.

Even now, outside of India, when one Indian meets another, the first question you ask, after you have gauged her or his geographical coordinates by their first name and last name, is "Which part of India are you from?" Then, "Oh, I thought so; your name gave you away," and "Do you make idli/sambar?"

I could go on all day about how we pick and gamble on people's identities. One day, I hope to see us connecting with each other as individuals first, rather than a person from a particular region. What if one hasn't lived up to the indicators that particular region is known for? What if you chose a state or region that you are not born into, but have adopted? Does that make you a traitor? As much as I have seen change happen as people cross state lines, blending in, marrying into different faiths and regions, or just relocating themselves to a part of India they love, we still have a long way to go. We still have paths to walk on.

# 12

# *My Father, the Merchant*

《 》

**I** SAW MY FATHER ONLY ONCE IN MY LIFE.

My father was my maternal uncle's friend. They were colleagues, and were posted on a job in our hometown. My uncle persuaded my grandfather to give a room on rent to my father when he came to work. My mother had just come back to the town she grew up in after being away at college in a different city. It was love at first sight, people said.

Unbeknownst to her parents (my grandparents), my mother and father decided that they wanted to be together and they wanted to get married. It was not easy. My father was a Hindu Punjabi, and my mother was a Christian of mixed heritage. My mother and her siblings were raised as Christians. Faith and religious affiliations played a very important part in the family.

I don't know much about why my grandfather's leanings towards Christianity were so strong and so unaccepting of other faiths. His mother was a Hindu who had eloped to marry his Christian father. Yet in his home, there was no tolerance or place for any of his children or grandchildren to marry into households of a different faiths. Love was frowned upon by him, even though he set sail for foreign shores in the early 1900s and came back home with a bride who was of a different culture, different color, and different race. They did not even speak the same language. The only thing they had in common was their Christianity. My grandmother was raised in the Orthodox Russian Church and my grandfather was a Baptist.

I don't know if it was a sign of the times, or basic intolerance, or just the era he belonged to. He wanted all his seven children, and later in life, all his twenty-one grand children, to agree to an arranged marriage. And if it was not arranged, the only marriage he would accept was if the partner was Christian. For the two of us who rebelled and married outside our faith, religion, and culture, we were ostracized for a long time.

*Your father approached me several times, for permission to marry your mother, but I refused to agree to the marriage of a Christian girl with a non-Christian. Your father was a Hindu and did not even believe in the existence of God. Anyway they agreed to be married against my opposition. I could not prevent it. Your mother was a grown-up girl and educated enough. I give advice and counsel and not force myself on others. So on the 1st of*

*August, 1956 they were married at home according to the Christian Marriage Act. Earlier to the ceremony I had left the house and returned long after it was over.*

After they got married, my father was transferred out of our hometown and went to live in a city a few states removed. There is not much information about their married life. No one spoke to kids; you just gathered information as you went along. Trouble seemed to have set in early in the marriage, according to my grandfather's notes. I have heard of my father being called a gambler by different people in our family. It seems he sold the furniture my grandfather, who finally relented, gave them for their wedding. The gold jewelry that my mother was given was also sold. Like so many other things in my life, I will never know the truth behind all this.

What I do see, though, or at least with the writings of my grandfather, is a cold, heartless person emerge from this elusive, mysterious person who was my father. He appears and he disappears, snatches and claims, and rides heartless over people's feelings and emotions. For the first two years of my life and the first six years of my brother's life, when we lived with our mother in her hometown after she left my father for the first time, he kept coming and going. Uprooting us as and when he chose.

*Your father and your brother left by the night train on October 27th 1962 . . . Our heart broke to part with your brother. He was very attached to me. After the train left I cried bitterly for him and repented myself why I allowed him to go away. Had I been aware of the events which occurred a few years later I would have never parted with him.*

I was a year and a half, and my brother five. My father was back again in our hometown with my brother in May of 1963. After staying for a few days, he left again, this time leaving my brother behind.

*A few days after the departure of your father, you mother went away leaving you and your brother with us. Your mother's behavior and neglect of you had become intolerable to us. At one time I made her leave the home. She would go out all evenings and would remain away from home for days together.*

*Then suddenly your mother and father arrived in Cuttack on the 2nd of July, 1963 and told me they had come to take you all back to Delhi. I was very happy on your account though I was sad to part with you. My love for you had to be subordinated to my desire to see your father owning you and accepting you as his child.*

Six days later on the eighth of July, 1963, it seems my parents, my brother, and I were on a train to Delhi. New Delhi is in the north of India, and is India's Capital, while Cuttack is in Orissa on the Eastern side of India. Both these places distant from each other in miles, language, culture, climate, and food.

*Your departure was a shock to me,* writes my grandfather.
*I was filled with sorrow in my heart. The only happiness I
have was that you have gone to your father who had once
denied you.*

In September of 1963, my grandfather came to Delhi to
visit us.

*I used to watch your father's attitude towards you. Even
though he was fonder of your brother. He was also loving
towards you and carried you around. I thought the relationship between your parents and your father's attitude
towards you had considerably improved and that all will be
well in the future. I then decided to return to Cuttack after
ten days. My short sojourn with you all in Delhi made me
feel that you will not be rejected by your father and that his
earlier attitude towards you must have changed. I felt all
will be well in the future, little knowing that a shock was
waiting for me within two months. Now I think that to
impress me he was showing such love and care, which were
not genuine.*

In January of 1964, I still had not turned three, and my
mother wrote to my grandfather to come and take me away
because we no longer were a family unit. My father had
taken my brother and gone, and here I was, left by the way-
side either to be picked up by the highest bidder or someone
with a heart.

That was the last that I "saw" of my father. I had no con-
crete images of his face or his voice. I had no recollection of

my brother, either. They both had disappeared from my life, with no memories to hold on to, just a bunch of pictures and notes kept diligently by my grandfather, which I did not have access to for a long time to come. When I did get to them years later, and went through the album, I saw he had labeled each picture with the names: Bubu's (my nickname) Father, Mother, Brother. That was my introduction to my family.

Some days I sneaked some pictures off to school, hoping and praying that he would not find them missing while I was gone. If he did, I knew one of the canes would come out, and like they say in India, I would have got a motherless thrashing. I was willing to take that risk. Always coveting other people's lives, parents, and lifestyles, I had to show my friends that I did have parents, I did have a brother, and that the three of them were not a figment of my imagination.

As a child, the future is not important. All I wanted to do was live in the present. But my present was full of restrictions and frugality. I grew up always feeling like the underdog, that I always missed out on fun, and that I seemed to be a dead weight on light, easy to break shoulders. Self-pity, I seemed to have a bunch, especially when I was young. I was always a tragedy-stricken princess in my mind and in all the plays and scenes that I enacted in my head.

❲ ❳

In April of 1977, I turned sixteen. A few days after that, I came back from school one day to see someone standing on our balcony on the first floor looking towards the road I would be on walking back from school. He was a complete stranger. Fair, not very tall, muscular, and young, I did not know who he was. As I walked up the steps, I brushed past him to see both my grandparents sitting on the verandah. I was a moody, insolent, and sometimes bratty teenager. I did not communicate with my grandparents much, except when I needed something or if there was something important to share. My grandfather looked at me, and asked, "Do you recognize him?" No, I had never seen him before. My first thought was, maybe it was some neighbor's kid who had come to complain about how my friends and I had snuck into their orchard to steal mangoes? Many a complaint had been filed about how unruly and bad I was for a girl!

"That is your brother, Pintu. See this picture, of him on the scooter and you sitting behind him? That is him. He is your bhaiya (older brother) and that is what you should call him."

Little did my grandfather know how familiar I was with that picture. Little did he know how many times I had talked with that picture. Talking to that picture about my crushes, my bad grades, my desire to travel and play with my cousins, and so many other myriad conversations. But those conversations were beyond long ago. They were filed under "foolish thought," and kept away. They disappeared the day I realized that I was on my own.

*Pintu & Bubu*

*Cuttack, August. 1962*

*With my brother.*

On seeing my brother for the first time when I was six-teen, there were no Bollywood movie moments, no song playing in the background. It was ironic, though, a few years before he showed up in my life, there was a Bollywood movie released about a brother and sister who were separated when they were young and found each other when they were adults. There is a song in that movie that the brother sings: "Pholon ka taaron ka, sab ka kehena hai, ek hazaaro mein mere behena hai" (The flowers and the stars all say that my sister is one in a thousand). I would sing this song many a time in my tragic princess moments.

My brother stayed a week. It was a week of turmoil and discomfort. I could not really connect with him. He was twenty, and I was sixteen. He seemed to be filled with bitterness and anger. He hated my mother, and hated the Samuels, who for some reason he thought were responsible for everything that had gone wrong in his life. He worshipped my father, and walked around singing his praises all the time. This very father who, when my brother was ten, had remarried and gave in to his wife, who told him that my brother was studying in too expensive a school and that they should pull him out and have him study in a less expensive school. This very father who, when at twelve my brother had run away from home and was living off the streets and god knows doing what, had not done a thing to go look for his son. My brother did not go back to my father till he was nineteen. He had no education, but had skilled himself in martial arts and made a living off that.

When at twenty he came to Cuttack, he was angry, jealous and sometimes mean. He thought I was the lucky one between the two of us and that he had gotten a bad deal. Yet, his father was his hero.

One of the days he asked me, "Do you want to go meet my father?" My father, he said, not our father.

I wanted to go meet the man whose name was on my birth certificate. I wanted to meet the man who I thought on seeing me would hug me and say what a pretty daughter he had, or how much he had missed me or regretted not seeing me grow up.

Apparently my father was back in Cuttack on work. He did not live there, but had a few clients there. We met at a general store that was owned by one of his clients. As we walked in, I recognized him from my album. A little heavier, a little greyer, but there he was, the same square jaw that I thought I had inherited from him. He was talking to someone and turned around to acknowledge my brother with a nod. I stood there, looking around, and eventually sat on a chair.

He walked up to us, ran his hand over my brother's forehead, and gave me a tap on my shoulder with a slight smile.

"Do you want some ice-cream?"

"Sure," I said.

He signaled to the storekeeper, who sent across two.

While I sat and ate the cone, my brother and father walked a few steps away and huddled in a corner, talking.

After ten minutes, my brother came back and said it was time to go. I nodded and got up. And thus ended my interaction with the man who was supposed to be my father.

On our way back to my grandparents, my brother asked me, "So, after Papa and Granny die, who gets Moti Bhavan?" Till today, I wonder if the only reason my brother came to Cuttack and took me to meet my father was to see if I stood to inherit something. Maybe for my father, it was finally time to get that bribe. Again, it is one of those mysteries in my life that I will never be able to solve.

He died in 2000, was what I was told.

# PART III

# 13

# *Pretty*

⟨ ⟩

S A CHILD, I always seemed to have problems breathing. I slept with my mouth open and seemed to gasp with every breath. I ran sport and track, and represented my school in badminton, but did not ever get to be really good because I would always end up breathless. After several rounds of doctors, the conclusion drawn was that I had a deviated nasal septum and that the part of the septum that was deviated needed to be taken out for air to flow freely. A simple enough surgery. There was one hospital in Cuttack, which was also a medical school, and the surgeon who was going to do the surgery taught and worked at that hospital. I was fourteen. .

After the surgery, I stayed in the hospital for three days, bandages swaddling my face. My cousin, who was a student at the medical school, had been by my side through the surgery and the nights. On the fourth day, my bandages were due to come off.

The nurse came in, wheeling her cart with all the things she needed to remove the bandages. My grandparents, my cousin, and a few of her medical school friends stood around my bed while the nurse unwrapped my mummy-like face. I sat up on my bed, already dressed in my jeans and a polka-dotted shirt, dreaming of how I would represent my country as an ace badminton player.

As the nurse was cleaning my face with a strong antiseptic, oh how I hate that smell, the doctor walked in. I looked up at my cousin and the people surrounding me. On their faces were shock and horror. My grandmother sat down on my bed, and my grandfather walked out of the room.

"So good, you can breathe now," the doctor said. It wasn't a question. It was just a statement from a doctor. "Come see me in ten days."

No one said a word. No mirror was placed in front of me. I didn't know what was happening. My cousin, who was and always will be a softie, had tears in her eyes.

"Di, what happened?" I asked her.

"Don't worry, Bubs, it will be okay." The nurse went to her station and came back with a hand-held mirror.

I held it and looked into it.

The first thought that struck me was that while I was sleeping, a truck had run over the middle of my face and had flattened out my nose. I had no septum left. Having learned early in life not to cry in public, I held back every emotion I had. Weak from the surgery and the lack of solid food, I was silent as a stone.

A rickshaw was called and my grandmother sat with me while my grandfather headed home on his bicycle. No one said a word.

I was ashamed of my face. I was ashamed to go to school. I had started noticing boys. Boys noticed me. There was a flutter every now and then. I had been ashamed to be part of a family that was known for their Greco-Roman noses. I was a misfit, physically.

After staying home for a week, I could no longer avoid going to school. So I put a Band-Aid on my nose, hoping to cover up the part where my nose used to be. The Band-Aid was not clay. It didn't fix or bring back what I had.

I walked all the way to school with my head down. I made it. The boys who stood waiting near the school pond or the large oak tree just to glance at girls that they had a crush on were there when I walked in. My heart skipped a beat and dropped ten beats. I walked past them, and into my class.

My deskmate was already there. She looked up, said hello, and her eyes stopped midway on my face. I saw the reflection in her eyes. Shocked, questioning, and a little bit of discomfort. Pity came later. We never talked.

At recess, the boys would usually swing by to say hi. No one came that day. I sat stoic in class in the second row, all day, from 8:30 A.M. to 3:30 P.M., wondering what they were saying behind my back.

A month or two before my surgery, a boy had come from another city to stay with us for three days. Along with a friend, he was taking an entrance exam in one of the local colleges in Cuttack. He was seventeen, and was known to the family, and hence considered "safe" to be a houseguest. My heart fluttered when I saw him. He was young, good looking, and wore the trendiest clothes I had seen. He seemed to like me too. We got along well ,with him regaling me with stories of a city so far removed from mine. The day he left I was bereft.

"I will be back for you. Don't run away. And don't crush all those hearts with those eyes of yours." This was the first time a boy had said anything like this to me.

Meanwhile, my grandfather was looking into this alliance. For him, this person was God-sent. Here was someone he could hand over my responsibility to when I came of age. He began corresponding with the parents of the boy, and it was decided that at seventeen, we would be married.

After he left, we wrote to each other almost every week. He would write to me about his new course in college, how his family liked my pictures, and how his dream was to join the Merchant Navy.

His dream took over my dreams. I looked forward to the day we would get married, how I would leave Cuttack, and how I would sail the oceans with him while he worked. I knew there would be no opposition to our getting married because he was from a good Christian family and was on his way to having a career that could support a family. I lived for the day and the new life I would get to live once I got married.

I had told him about the surgery that I was going to have. He was going to come again to Cuttack to take his finals for the course he was doing in about six months. The exam was scheduled at the end of March. Since my birthday was on the first of April, he had said he would stay an extra day or two to celebrate with me. My excitement knew no bounds.

He arrived in Cuttack in the early hours on the 29th of March. His exams were scheduled for the 30th and the 31st. I could hear him from my room talking to my grandmother, and telling her about his parents and how they asked about her. I could hear the impatience and the anticipation in his voice. He was waiting for me.

I walked into the dining room. He looked up with a smile, and in a second, that smile faded. Faded into a face that expressed horror. Faded into an expression of disbelief. I saw discomfort in his eyes and heard disappointment in his voice when he said, "Hello, how are you?"

"I am fine." My face was my face. Since the surgery, I had learned to live with it. I could not do away with my face.

Much of the day he spent studying in his room for his exams, only coming out for food. The next evening he announced that he would be leaving to go back on the thirty-first, straight from the center where he was taking his exams. Apparently he forgot that he had to be back for a prior commitment.

I knew that would be the last I would see of him. There were no tears, no questions, just acceptance. A week after he went back, I got a letter from him. When I looked at that envelope, the familiar address from where it was coming, his beautiful handwriting, and the stamp from his local post office, my heart no longer did its familiar jump-with-joy beat. I imagined him going to drop it off. My heart sank. I knew this was my eviction notice.

# 14

# *New Delhi*

《 》

LIVING IN A SMALL TOWN, there were a lot of things that girls could not do after a certain age. One could never venture out of the house without an escort, and couldn't wear jeans or any other outfit that would make you look a) like a boy, or b) too promiscuous. C) God forbid if a prospective groom's parent or family saw you like that! There went all your chances marrying a boy from a good family who would make sure you were comfortably taken care of, and best of all, that you did not have to work.

Yes, that was what most of us had to strive towards, and look forward to, and achieve. For those of us who had the label "comes from a broken family" on their foreheads, the chances were slim. No one wanted to take the risk of marrying their son off to a girl who might do the same thing her parents did, and get a divorce.

Society was not kind, and is still not kind, to girls and women, in any kind of role they play. A woman or a girl, especially from my part of the world, is as soon as she is old enough to stand up and walk accompanied either by the father, the brother, a male cousin, or a friend's son who has been vetted and certified to be a safe bodyguard. Never is she alone, never can she say, "Leave me alone, I need my space."

It is in the name of love, and it is stifling. I remember very early in life being told that "a girl does not swing her hands when she walks," that "when you walk on the streets, don't lift your head up," to "make sure people don't notice you on the roads," to "behave yourself, you are a girl." Don't open your mouth and laugh, you are a girl. You are a girl, you are a girl, you are a girl.

> *You spend more time playing and quarreling with your boy cousin and whatever he does you imitate him. He is a boy and he can be excused for being naughty, but you are a girl and you are expected to be calm and sober by nature. I am very perturbed about your general behavior. You want to play and fight all the time. Your cousin is a boy and rowdyism on his part can be excused, but you are a girl and this sort of behavior on your part is unforgivable.*

From early childhood, a girl is taught and indoctrinated to examine herself continually. She has to survey everything she is and everything she does, because how she appears to the world, and especially to men, could make or break her future. Too much makeup makes her look like a slut. Talking a lot makes people think she is too talkative.

In my first year at college, when I turned seventeen, my grandfather, who saw that people were not lining up at his gate to ask for my hand in marriage, decided to rectify the situation by getting me to have another surgery. This time he did a little research and narrowed it down to a plastic surgeon who came highly recommended by a family doctor friend who also had a nursing home. Once again, I was prepped for surgery. I was hopeful. Maybe I would become pretty again.

( )

Two nights later, the bandages came off and I looked in the mirror. Once again, I knew I could never be pretty again. There was no magic performed by this gifted plastic surgeon. I don't think he knew what he needed to do to fix me.

So my grandfather started reaching out to his Christian network. Friends and friends of friends were recruited to find a good boy for me. One day, he seemed to finally have found someone. An old friend's daughter, who was also my mother's classmate in school, was married outside of Cuttack and had three boys. The oldest was a few years older than me and was studying to be an engineer. Through letters it was decided that we would get engaged, and in a year or two, we would be married. At nineteen, we had a long-distance engagement. The families had known each other for almost two generations and there was no checking-out that needed to be done.

I was beginning to have hope again. Romance was not dead. Since he lived in another town, there was no question of dating or going out; writing letters to each other was the only communication allowed. His distance made it easy to follow the "rules." Every three days I would wait for the postman to walk up with a letter for me from him. I lived for those letters. From a very early age, I think marriage seemed to be the only path out of the life that I had. So, I lived for that day. Lived for the excitement of everything that came along with it. My saris were bought, my jewelry was made, and pots and pans were being collected for my trousseau.

A month before our wedding, the boy wrote, saying he realized that he loved someone else and needed to be with her. I was devastated. But growing up, I was told that girls weren't supposed to get dramatic, loud, or agitated. I suffered in silence, pretending all was right with the world.

❮ ❯

In 1980, I finished my bachelor's degree in English literature. Most of my fellow graduating friends were either getting ready to be married to a boy their parents had chosen for them, or were going on to complete their masters.

Born into a culture that overwhelmingly favored arranged marriages, letting your grown daughter move out of sight, or move to another town, was not something that people from my race did or do easily. Marriage was the only honorable way out for a daughter of a marriageable age. And that magical age was between seventeen and twenty-one in most families. After that magical year crossed over into the unmagical year, questions would begin to be asked, aspersions would begin to be cast. And with a culture that thinks women and girls are a responsibility, it was always the girl who bore the brunt of these unsettling thoughts.

That is when the wheels of culture, responsibility, and of course, concern for your child, were set into motion. Both the boy's family and the girl's family would have a set of private investigators—mostly family friends, business associates, and extended family members—who would take it upon themselves to investigate the "candidate" and report back whether the match was considered suitable.

If the boy was being investigated, his income, his education, his hierarchy within his family, his lifestyle, and the kind of friends he had came under scrutiny. For a girl, it was her skin color, her education, her ambitions (she should not have her own, her future husband's ambition should be her priority), whether she had boyfriends, her culinary abilities, how she spoke and communicated, and the kind of clothes she wore (hopefully not too revealing or modern). The common belief was that marriage in itself was a huge commitment and adjustment, and marrying into your own faith, culture, and social status just made things easier. Somehow, between all these checks and balances, the compatibility of a couple was never a checkpoint.

I knew marriage was not one of my options. When you are not allowed to have boyfriends, your only option is to wait for your parents to find a boy for you. For this, all the odds were stacked against me. My grandparents were too old to even think about going through the tedious process, and my aunts and uncles had their own children to worry about. I was a child of divorced parents with a question mark about who my father was. And my physical appearance had none of the attributes that a prospective groom's family was looking for. The only option to me at that time was to get an education in a field that I really wanted to pursue.

After almost a six-month struggle with my grandfather, who it seemed just wanted me to stay home and lie in wait for a proposal to come by, I finally wore him down to send me to the capital of India, New Delhi, to study. Of course not without accusations, recriminations, and regrets of all the sacrifices he had made on my behalf and for me. He lamented the day he took me in, and told me how I was crushing all his dreams, and this would not be the first time he said that. Delhi was a big, bad city. Only people with low moral standards went there or lived there. Delhi was the big bad wolf that would eat me alive.

Till today, I still don't know how he gave in. Without him consenting, I would never have left my hometown. There was no such thing as "I am an adult; I can do what I want." There was no concept of student loans that I could rely on. It had to be your parents or grandparents supporting you. But give in, he finally did, even though I was like the proverbial frog in a well. I jumped out of the well and found the courage to get on that train, and it took me away to the big, bold city of New Delhi. It was the summer of 1981.

I lived for my first few months in the college hostel. With the oppressive Delhi summers, living on the top floor, where they had created makeshift rooms with a tin roof for the late admissions to school, turned out to be difficult and isolating. There were three of us up there. And as luck would have it, all three of us came from towns that almost no one in our college had ever heard of. Round one to the unknowns and the unseens. Coming from not-so-privileged financial backgrounds, the three of us knew from the onset that we could never be one of "them," with their in-style wardrobes, their fancy book bags, and the even fancier cars that came to drop them off and pick them up.

The boarders, who lived on the floor below us, were not very inclusive. With money and parental support on their side, they had already figured out how not to deal with the meager meal plan that the hostel provided. Instead, they found a local woman who would cook almost whatever they wanted.

I was a misfit from the get-go. My clothes were at least three years behind in their vintage. No, vintage clothes were not trendy then! And after my nose surgery, even my looks felt in the losing category. No one went out of their way to befriend me. I guess if your face is not perfect, that reflects on your perfection. No one wanted to be in a place where their social wellbeing could be jeopardized.

Envy and jealousy were beginning to take over me. All I wanted to be was one of those pretty girls who had everything going for them: the families, the boys swooning behind them, and the confidence they had to face the world on their own terms. I found myself always snooping, trying to figure out how their lives seemed so glamorous and fun all the time. I longed to be part of their little cliques and conversations. A polite smile would be all I got from them when I tried to ingratiate myself in their midst. I would come away every single time feeling slighted and lost.

Delhi. This was the very city where I had spent the first two years of my life with my parents. And they owned and lived in one of those very same homes that I coveted from afar. The home still existed when I went back to that city at twenty-one. And like everything that is ironic in my life, it was in the same neighborhood as my college. Could I tell them, "Guess what, that three-story building that you see across the road, with the man standing guard near the gate, with the board that says, 'Singh Nivas'? That was/is my home. I played within those walls. I ate, drank, slept, and played within those walls. Now do you like me better, knowing that I come from money?" But those words could never come out of my mouth.

With almost all my energy being spent on feeling inadequate and not fitting in, I decided to ask a distant aunt if she would be willing to take me in as a paying guest while I finished my studies. She agreed, and the next day I packed my bags and moved to her home. Far from eyes that judged or opinions that crushed, I found myself slowly regaining the purpose that I had when I moved to Delhi. It did not matter that my room in my aunt's home was the space under the steps. As tiny as it was, I made it mine for the time I lived there. My bed was my desk, my sleep space, my ironing board, and my escape. There, I felt accepted and included.

All I had now was my advertising world. I had to embrace it, and feel it to feel alive again. I had aspirations of joining an advertising agency on Madison Avenue. The advertising industry in India in those days had still not come of age, and the examples we followed in class were mostly out of agencies in New York. Needless to say, that's where I thought my talent would blossom. Sitting on my front steps, I looked at the skies and wondered if the skies in New York looked the same.

My only dream then was to be one of the million people whom I had seen (in movies) walking the crowded streets of New York. I would be in my blue Levi's jeans (it was a craze), carrying a brown paper bag full of groceries, walking up to my apartment back from my advertising school. I would stop somewhere for coffee and sandwiches, read my Advertising Age, and think what a wonderful life I had. I needed the wide-open roads, the bluest of skies, the snowiest roads—all of that seemed picture-perfect in postcards that friends or family from beyond my little town's horizons sent me. Going to America was my dream. I could reach out and catch it. Each morning, I took the bus to my college and walked in with a little more confidence than I had before.

# 15
# *Death of a Dream*

❨ ❩

ARLY 1983, I finished my degree in advertising and public relations. I was ready to go out and conquer the world, armed with this piece of paper that told people I was creative and could sell ideas. I was a brand-new person. Then I decided to return to my hometown and give up my dreams.

Till today, I do not know why I did this. I suppose I knew that in the big city, I would be lost with nothing but my degree on my side. The ability to speak up and play rebel all disappeared when practicality struck. There was no longer a hostel in which to stay, like while I was studying. I would have to find a place to live that would be affordable on my meager intern's paycheck. My grandfather had refused to send me money to help supplement my income, so I could either go back home or be like a "prostitute on the streets of Delhi."

Come back home to Cuttack is what I did. I no longer had the strength to fight. I had resigned myself to my fate. The dreaded, sinking feeling that I had carried in my heart came back with a blast, like the heat of a hot summer day. With the windows shut and the coir mats hung, dripping with water, to cool the bedrooms and keep the heat out, summers in India are still treacherous and long. By 11:00 A.M., the towns come to a standstill. The oppressive heat keeps everyone indoors for most parts of the day, till the light summer breeze comes along around six in the evening.

In Cuttack, cooped up in a house of five bedrooms with two old people, my future seemed bleak and dark. I had nothing to look forward to. No parents of boys came knocking on our doors to ask for my hand in marriage, and there was no trousseau shopping for saris, gold jewelry, household goods, or beautiful cosmetics or perfumes like other parents had started gathering. No out-of-town trips to a bigger city to buy the latest saris for the wedding. There was nothing. I felt stifled, and the rooms seemed to close in on me. Was it just a year ago that I was blissfully happy in a city far away?

With Cuttack hardly having any options in terms of a career, a friend circle, or anything uplifting, I began studying German with the hope that my aunt in Germany would sponsor me to go live and work there. My friends from college had either moved to larger cities to study and work or were married, so I stayed home all day doing much of nothing, and three days a week in the evenings, my grandfather would walk me to a local college for my classes.

As much as I loved learning a new language, I knew it wasn't going anywhere. My aunt in Germany had written to my grandfather saying she could not take the responsibility of a young girl. I continued going for the classes and taking all the qualifying exams for two specific reasons: 1) I had nothing else to do, and 2) I thought this would make me a little more marketable in the marriage market.

Life was lonely. Then, in January of 1984, there was an ad in the newspaper. It was for a local advertising agency in Cuttack. They were looking for a copywriter. I applied, and they scheduled an interview. I was excited, and thought life was finally looking up. I went for the interview with my grandfather standing guard outside, and met with the four owners of the agency, who were all related. My grandfather came in too, and met with my prospective bosses. They hired me on the spot. Even if I must say so myself, I was quite a novelty in the Cuttack of the mid-Eighties.

I was excited, finally feeling like a human being who had something to look forward to. I had something to contribute to the world, and I could finally use and justify the degree that I had earned.

I took a rickshaw to work every morning, and in the evenings, my grandfather walked the three miles to my workplace, waited till I finished, and walked me back home. At the end of the month when I got my paycheck, which was actually cash, my joy knew no bounds. I don't remember contributing towards the running of the household, but I took over my expenses, buying a lipstick or a nail polish or new clothes, something which was a rarity when I did not have money.

Things, however, were not always calm. There were always hidden innuendoes. I was the only woman who had dared to go work with a bunch of men for a living. The tiny town that I lived in had its own set of rules that were acceptable. Judging was something that people seemed to do for a living. And I had so much to be judged on. I was a Christian (the undercurrents of that day and age were that Christian girls had loose morals), I had no parents, and I didn't seem to be in the zone or the platform of being accepted by a family for marriage. So if I went out for meetings or to meet clients, it must be because I was desperate and needed someone to hook up with. The judging eyes would follow me if at work I got into a car with my boss, or, if the car came to drop me off at home after a day of client meetings, the eyes would follow me from the car to the gate and bore into me.

Some days, even before I came home, my grandfather would have already known what time I left the office and what mode of transport I had taken and with whom. He seemed to cringe with all this unnecessary attention. The only thing normal about this situation was his sense of denial that his family was perfect, and that they did not have any skeletons in their cupboard, and that the whole world did not know what was going on. He had been in denial ever since his oldest, unmarried daughter died in London a few days after giving birth to a baby. He was in denial when he was raising me ten doors down from his youngest daughter, whom he had banished from our home and who happened to be my mother. It was a house full of secrets and denials.

But whatever the outside world seemed to be doing grew my grandfather's determination to find me a good, Christian boy by leaps and bounds, though my own faith in Christianity was waning for no fault of the faith; I did not understand a faith that had allowed no tolerance. As his discomfort grew about my being out there in the world, working and being in a place that according to him was vulnerable to "bad men," so did his determination to get me married.

The first proposal that came for me was from a young gentleman who attended prayer meetings with my grandfather and was deeply embedded in his Pentecost faith. I had never talked to him in my life, and the only time or two that I had seen him was when he came to our home when my grandfather hosted the prayer meetings. I was never part of the meetings, but would hear them all the way in my room, trying to part the heavens with their loud prayers and their speaking in tongues.

I had a vision of what my life was going to be if I said yes. He had one glass eye. At twenty-three, even though I had a disfigured face that I covered most of the time with large, hideous eyeglasses, I was vain, and still expected a tall, dark, and handsome man to sweep me off my feet. I guess I did not look into the mirror much in those days. Life can be ironic in many ways.

The noose seemed to be getting tighter and tighter. The burden of being a young girl with grandparents in their dotage was proving to be heavy on all our shoulders. With no sign of a future that I had envisioned, most days I felt cornered and trapped.

# 16

# *A Proposal*

❪ ❫

ONE OF MY FOUR BOSSES, Arun, was the creative director of the company. He was an artist, had studied in New York, and was also the art director for a few regional movies. He was not married, and apparently had a host of girlfriends, according to office gossip. His day job was as the head of the advertising and marketing department of a textile factory, and after work he drove up to the ad agency on his motorcycle to finish his creative assignments or work on portraits he was painting. Every stroke of his brush and color on a blank canvas made me stare in awe.

Through the office grapevine, I had also learned that Arun was in love with this girl from his college days, a girl he wrote poems about and whose portraits he painted. Her family turned him down the first time he asked for her hand in marriage because he was not a doctor like his older brother who lived in America, and was just a college graduate with a bachelor's degree. He walked away from her, took a plane to America, and went to SUNY in Albany to do his MBA. For four years he never looked back. He went on to complete his MBA, got commissioned to paint the town hall in Albany, played soccer for his university team, and worked part-time as a bartender.

After graduating, Arun decided to go back to India. His older brother, who lived in the US, had started the process of applying for his Green Card. Not too keen to stay on, and knowing that the immigration process could take years, Arun went back to India to work and maybe wait for the time to come for him to emigrate, and also to be with his widowed mother who lived by herself.

People in Cuttack were in awe of him. Here he was, "foreign returned" with a degree, an immensely talented man with a string of broken hearts tattooed on his arm. This fascinated twenty-three-year-old me. I had never met anyone like him in my life. I would watch him get into his creative zone, and be spellbound by his talent. The gratitude and self-worth that I felt when he asked me for my input on any creative process filled holes in my psyche.

I was fascinated how women—his friends and extended family—all spoke about him like he was a demigod, and like whatever quirks he had were part of his being so creatively brilliant. Everyone also seemed to be in awe of the fact that he had put his life on hold, and everything that he had going for him in America, to come back to his hometown. In that age, no one ever came back once they left. A reverse migration process was unheard of. America was still the land of dreams and achievements.

Some afternoons or evenings, the girl he had loved and who he had wanted to marry would come by. She was soft-spoken and lovely, and because she had known him since they were teenagers, she was also very comfortable with him, his mother, and his extended family. She and the friends or siblings she brought along as chaperones would all sit around with the four owners of the ad agency and chat over endless cups of tea and snacks. These interactions fascinated me. The depth of her love for him, and how far back they went with each other, was very evident in their interactions.

Even though there was no public display of emotions, their bond was very clear for everyone to see. While stories of their deep love, and his writing a screenplay and producing a movie that was based on her, did the rounds, what also circulated was how stubborn and full of pride he was. Once rejected, people said, even though he loved her, he would never marry her, because the first time around she did not have the courage to stand up to her parents.

And then on the other side was she. She had stopped combing her hair the day he flew out of India to go study in America, and had promised she would only comb out her knots once he returned and they got married. So here she was, a head full of knots, and love and devotion flowing out of every pore. It seems he chose not to get married because his heart was ripped out by her when she let him leave. Always a sucker for love stories, I was enthralled by their life. I wanted to be loved and love someone the way they did each other.

Once in a while, Arun would come over to my desk and start chatting, basically asking about my life, where I had studied, and what else I liked to do. There were days he would take me for client meetings on his motorcycle. Those were the days that Bollywood movie songs and scenes would seep into my head. I would imagine being the heroine and singing songs like they did on the silver screen.

Some days I would hear his cousins say to him that he needed to get married, and that he needed to close out all the half-read chapters in his life. The more people pushed him, the more he seemed to dig his heels in and not move towards this girl he loved. I did not see this as strong ego, or being stubborn and full of pride; I just saw him as someone who had loved deeply and was too hurt to let it go.

Some days we talked, just him and me. He was so full of stories and anecdotes, and passionate about arts and culture. It drew me in. This dearth of stimulating conversation that I'd had most of my life suddenly seemed to disappear. He paid attention, he let me talk, and he listened to what I had to say, though with not too many experiences or exposures to talk about, I would mainly listen and be the demure girl I was supposed to be.

Three months into my working at the agency, it was my birthday and we were supposed to go meet a client. Arun was also going across town to do a photo shoot. Did I mention that he was an amazing photographer, and that the kit he had was something that a want-to-be photographer like me, who had studied photography as a subject and had learned how to operate a dark room, deeply coveted? Since I was going the same direction, he asked me if I wanted to ride with him. "Yes," I said. "Sure thing."

After meeting with the client, we went to the location of his shoot. He was taking pictures of Rock Edicts from the era 269 BCE to 232 BCE that stood on the banks of a river where a famous Indian emperor had embraced Buddhism after seeing the bloodshed in the infamous Kalinga War.

While the sun started setting beyond the Dhauli Hills, as he stood, taking pictures of the sunset, Arun turned to me, and said, "I like you, will you marry me?"

Not even a split second or a blink of an eyelid did it take me to answer. "Yes." All coy and shy with my head focused on my feet. Wow, he likes me, he will write poems about me, he will make a movie about me, he who was so fascinating with all the stories that he told me about the years he studied in America, the girlfriends he had, the escapades in the bar that he tended, the myriad other life experiences that he had, would finally be how I lived my life. That was all I thought about at that minute. There was also a sense of misplaced pride. Maybe he had chosen me over the girl who pined for him and was still waiting for him. I am not sure why, but there was a sense of victory.

That was it. In India, especially in the early 1980s, one never hugged or kissed in public. We got into the car and the driver drove us back to the office. Our hands briefly touched in the back seat. That was our first physical contact. The only thing that was decided before we stepped back into the car was not to tell anyone in the office or anyone in our respective families for just now. I was fine with that. I was petrified about my grandfather's reaction.

# 17
# Telling the Families

《 》

APRIL ROLLED INTO MAY, and May brought on the summer heat of June in more ways than one. Arun and I hardly ever met outside the office, because that would mean the whole world finding out, and continued working as if nothing had happened.

In early June, he told me that his brother and family were arriving from America and that he wanted me to meet them in New Delhi before they came to Cuttack. He had briefly told his sister-in-law about me on the phone, but had not given her too many details. I was excited, and at the same time afraid, because I did not know how to go missing for a couple of days.

I told my grandparents that I needed to go to Delhi to pick up my diploma from the university, and promised them

I would stay with a cousin who lived there. Since I was working and had money of my own to buy my train ticket, I did not really need anything from my grandfather except permission to go. That permission was given after days of labored struggle and loud voices. Once again, the world was not safe for me to be out there by myself, and there was absolutely no need for me to go get my diploma in person, since it could always be mailed in.

With fuel of a different kind propelling me, I fought this one out and left for Delhi in the middle of June. Arun and I had decided not to start our travel from the same station, in case someone saw us board the train together. I got on one station before Cuttack, and he got on at Cuttack. We made the two-night journey to Delhi, oblivious to the fact that a family friend of my family had seen us inside the train compartment together and had immediately gone on to report this to my grandfather. I had no idea.

In Delhi, I stayed with Arun's brother and family at the guesthouse they had checked into. I spent two days with them, going shopping, eating out, and basically getting to know them. His two nieces were young, and it was fun showing them where I shopped when I lived and studied there. Delhi was, and still is, a shopper's paradise. More than anything, it felt wonderful to be a part of a family, to be normal, and to do normal things like most families did. This was something I had never done before. I was liking this new way of living and spending one's life.

The two days that I spent in Delhi with them were the most fun I'd had in almost all my life. I could go where I wanted to, I could walk the streets like I wanted to, and I could breathe the air out in the open. While there, it was decided by the brothers that since the older one was leaving in a month's time to go back to the States, we needed to be married in July or August before he left. I agreed and went along with their plans.

When they went shopping and bought me saris, I was thrilled. I had never worn something that expensive. They talked about the venue, the things they needed to buy, the people they needed to invite, and what dates would be best according to the Hindu calendar when everything was perfectly aligned. It was decided that his brother and wife would come to our home and ask my grandparents for my hand.

I don't remember anyone stopping to ask me what I thought of all these plans or if there was anything that I wanted to add. I don't remember being steamrolled either. I was just so used to other people making decisions about my life, that nothing seemed amiss.

The short sojourn in Delhi was over, and this time around, I flew back with them to our hometown. With great trepidation, I was getting ready to tell my grandparents that I was planning to get married the next month. I walked into our home around lunchtime, and saw my grandparents at their usual spot at our round dining table. The spot between them where I sat was symbolically empty. As soon as I walked in, I knew something was wrong.

"You have shamed me," said my grandfather. "I never expected this reward from you."

Then he left the table. I tried to talk to my grandmother, who just sat there in stony silence. No amount of tears rolling down my face would get her to talk to me. Not much of a talker myself, and absolutely not equipped to handle any kind of conflict, I walked into my room and spent the rest of the day there.

The next few days were spent the same way. Neither of my grandparents talked to me, and I did not have the courage to go talk to them. Love, feelings, and marriage were things we had never spoken about together.

Years later, I found a letter to me from my grandfather:

> *20.6.1984.*
> *What have you done? You had been so secretive, so sly, you have stabbed with a knife that I have borne. Now, today you have thrust a dagger on the same spot on my chest where as a baby you had urinated and passed stool the smell of which still lingers. What have you done? Is this the reward for all love & care bestowed on you for the past twenty-three years. With one shot you have killed two birds & that too at the same time on the last lap of our lives. Oh God. How to endure this.*

Most of the days after that were spent with neither of them talking to me. Sometimes my grandmother would tell me, "You are not thinking. Let's go to Pune and spend some time there with your cousins." Pune was a city in a different state in India.

Too late, was what I wanted to tell her. But I could not say anything. I do not even remember if I understood any of the pain they were going through. Looking back now, I try to get a sense of what they really wanted. It was not that they had these tremendous plans for me, or that they had found a match for me that was perfect in every sense of the word.

They had nothing. My days blended into the other like a carbon copy of the previous.

In the beginning of July, there came my proposal. They walked into our home, the older brother, his wife, and a cousin. My grandparents met with them reluctantly while I sat in my room, trying to listen in on the conversation.

They sang praises of their brother, how talented he was, how he would take care of me, and how they would make sure I lacked for nothing.

My grandfather listened and talked, while my grandmother cried.

"Your brother is a Hindu, my child is a Christian, and how will she fit in? She does not know anything about Hinduism and I know you will convert her. That will kill me."

"Your culture is different, our culture is different. She was raised very differently and will not be able to fit into a typical Oriya household."

"She has no parents. We raised her when her parents separated and divorced when she was hardly two years old. Will your conservative society accept that?"

"He is twenty years older than her, how are you going to bridge that gap?"

"Please leave. She is an adult, if she wants to walk over my old body and leave us behind bleeding, she can do that."

"I will not be a part of that, and my wife will not be a part of it also."

And that was how my formal wedding proposal ended. The one proposal that I dreamed of, that would come draped in silk, with flowers and sweets and with everyone and everything in harmony.

After they left, my grandfather just looked at me, a look that seared right through me. But as rebellion and a sense of desperation started seeping in, I looked right back at him and said, "I have to do it."

One of the many regrets I have today is not having the chance to explain to him why I did what I did. He carried with him to his grave the thought that I was rebellious and was just like my mother and never cared. If only I could tell him. After they left, an uncle was summoned, my cousin was called, and my aunt came from a different part of India to talk to me. A friend from college who had come back to our town for a few months came by every day to try and talk me out of it. "Shabby, he is so much older than you. How can you marry him?"

My uncle and cousin went a couple of times to meet with the brother. They tried to tell him to call the wedding off, that they were sure in a couple of years our marriage would break down because of the differences between us. They also made sure to tell them that no one from our family would come or participate, and that basically, I was on my own.

I look back now and think what a zombie I had become. I just existed. I did not participate in my life. The entire July was spent with a lot of tears, sullenness, silence, and suffocation.

# 18

# The Heartbreak

( )

*This day will remain till my death, a day written with blood oozing out of the dagger thrust into my heart by my child. Today she goes out of my arms into which she had jumped in the Dum Dum Airport on 14.1.1964. But she can never get out of my heart into which she had entered, till my death.*

THE DAY ON THIS NOTE IS AUGUST 4, 1984. This note was written in India by my grandfather, hence the date first, then the month. I did not get to read this letter till February of 1986, a few days after my grandfather passed away.

On August 4, 1989, I saw the sunlight stream through my window. It was a bright summer morning, and the curtains in my room billowed softly in the light breeze. Such a beautiful

*Note from Grandfather
on Wedding Day.*

and gorgeous morning it was. I lay in bed looking up at my ceiling, having been in this position most of the night. I did not want to look outside. Despite all the promises that a new day brings, I had spent most of the night crying. My world as I knew it was shunning me, was closing the doors on me. In a few hours, all that was love, comfort, sadness, and heartache would fall into a big black void. I lay motionless and frozen, unable to gather the courage to stop what was going to happen.

Much of the previous night was spent with my closest friend, a cousin, and my mother's sister. On this long verandah in our colonial-style home, my grandmother sat at one end of the verandah dabbing her eyes with her handkerchief and talking to herself without verbalizing anything. At the other end of the verandah were the four of us. I sat on a wicker chair, my friend sat on an inside ledge, my aunt held my hand and gently caressed it, and my cousin paced up and down.

I always hated being the center of attention, and here I was, with everyone's focus on me. Anger, harsh words, sensible talk, pros and cons—everything had failed to change my mind. Now it was time for them to plead and cajole. I sat motionless, listening to my family. The turmoil that had swept through everyone's lives because of me had created a black cloud over our home.

"Don't do it, mama," said my aunt in a soft voice, using an Indian term of endearment for girls.

I looked at her and cried, "I don't want to, but I have made a promise!"

"You are throwing your life away," she said.

My friend, someone who was close to my heart and is still close to my heart, said to me, "Shabby, don't do it. Let's talk. Come stay with me."

My cousin, who was still pacing, kept saying, "Bubs, leave Cuttack for a little bit. Think about it."

But I was adamant. The night before my wedding, my aunt tried once again. How could I tell her, I have never learned to say no? How could I tell her if I said no, then I would not know what was behind the door? I felt cornered and helpless. I knew somewhere deep down inside my heart that it was something I really did not want. I seemed to have no control over my mind. I seemed to be living outside my body. I did not seem to want to confront myself. What were my choices?

On August 4, 1984, I was twenty-three years, four months, and three days old.

August 4, 1984, was my wedding day.

The house had not stirred as yet. It was 7:00 A.M. There were four people in the house that morning: my grandfather, my grandmother, my aunt, and I. Each of us was ensconced in our own room.

I was afraid to get up and leave my room. I did not have the courage to face anyone in the house. I knew I was ripping the heart out of two people in their eighties. That memory and that action is something I have never been able to forgive myself for. Till today, I still see the hurt in their eyes, the tears on their cheeks, and the utter devastation I left behind when all I left behind were footprints leading out of the house.

I could hear my grandfather in his room, three rooms away. What was he thinking? Was he saying the words I had heard so many times over? Ungrateful child. You cannot go to Hindu homes, they will feed you the things that they have offered to their gods. And the Bible says you shall have no other gods before me." I heard his words.

How could I have told him, every time, it is not the fault in my stars? I wanted to be a person, I wanted to be a human, and I wanted to have friends whose lives were always so much smoother than mine. I wanted to have their mothers ask about me, ask about what I wanted to eat, tell me I was too thin or too plump. I wanted normal. I wanted to look into someone's eyes and see youth.

I did not want to be afraid all the time. I did not want to hear, "If we die, where will you go?" and "Study hard and be obedient, only then will our Lord look after you."

I wanted to be a normal four year old, swaying in her frocks and cancan dresses without a care in the world. I wanted to climb trees, play marbles, play football, hang with the boys, and play dolls with the girls.

How could I explain to my grandfather that by leaving, I was trying to choose a life for myself that would be different, that would let me live without feeling like a burden? Without feeling like I was an ungrateful child whether I put my left foot first or right foot first?

How could I tell him that there were probably other roads I could have taken, other paths that I could have chosen, but that I wasn't equipped to deal with life. I was not taught how to deal with life.

How could I tell him that I really didn't know where I was going, but what I knew with absolute certainty was that I no longer wanted the life I had led up to that point? I was fleeing, I know, abandoning the only ship I knew, following the same footsteps of abandonment that had brought me to their doorstep. But what could I do? I needed to find the person who I truly was, amidst the layers of hurt, helplessness, and shame.

# 19
# My Wedding Day

《 》

I HAD PUT MY MEAGER BELONGINGS TOGETHER. Meager for someone who was getting ready to leave her parent's home and go to the home of her husband and in-laws. Meager and bare for an Indian girl, according to the general standards. I owned six saris and had put them all in my suitcase. The saris were not new. My grandfather was a strong-willed man. I was marrying without his permission, nay, against his wishes. We were not on talking terms. There was no question of asking him, "Where is my stuff?" The trousseau that had been collected through the years lay in the attic at Moti Bhavan when I was getting married.

A few weeks earlier, I had gone out by myself to buy a sari for my wedding with the monthly paycheck of five hundred rupees I had kept aside for my trousseau shopping. My wedding sari, which was cheap and shiny because that was all that I could afford, cost me two hundred and fifty rupees. It was red and had zari (brocade) on it that could blind anyone who came within a foot of me. I had nothing else—no gold jewelry to my name, like all lucky Indian girls should have, no brand new pots and pans, no fridge, no makeup, no perfumes, nothing to take with me. I had a few old salwar-kameez's (Indian clothes) that I packed, and that was it. I don't think I even wore new shoes or sandals on my wedding day.

I was ashamed. Ashamed to carry that old suitcase with me that had nothing in it. I remember folding every garment, and my tears falling into the creases and folds. I was desolate and sad. This was supposed to be the happiest day in a girl's life. Here I was, starting it out with tears and a sense of acute loss and alienation.

No wedding songs blared from the speakers that should have been affixed on the terrace of our home, no shamianas (tents), no family or extended family members coming days before the wedding to participate in the celebrations. No one calling the to-be bride over for kania dakras (for a meal) where there would be food and gifts for the wedding, and a lot of teasing would happen. No extended shopping sprees to buy bangles and bindis (the dot in between the eyebrows that Indian women use) with friends or cousins. No calling of a local cook and his staff to make pits in the backyard where food would be cooked by the kilos for anyone who came to visit or wish. There were no celebrations.

I don't even remember if my aunt walked me to the gate

that morning. I knew my grandparents would not come out of their respective rooms. I walked up to my grandfather's room, stood at the door, and said, "Papa, I am leaving." No answer, dead silence.

I then walked to my grandmother's room. She was still lying in her bed under the mosquito net. I did not lift the net, like I had done so many times growing up to either give her a kiss or to tell her something, I just bent down and said, I am leaving. We never said I love you growing up. I don't know if it was a hemispheric gag in that day and age, or if it was just our family. Today I so wish I could have said those three words to her and not left her so bereft.

I put on my red, shiny sari and was ready by nine for the car sent by my future in-laws to pick me up and drive me straight to a dak bungalow (guest house) about twenty miles away on the banks of a local river. I was told by a representative, a distant cousin of their family who had taken on the role of a messenger, that we would be getting married there by a judge. It was going to be a registered marriage. That fact had given me a little solace, because of the hundred recriminations and the "You will be sorry" that my grandfather had thrown at me. One of them was the fact that if we got married the Hindu way, circling the fire seven times to symbolize the wish that you want to be married to the same person for seven lifetimes, our marriage would not be legal because I was a Christian, and he a Hindu, and one could not marry people of different faiths in a religious or cultural way. The children I might have would have been considered illegitimate. So I was happy that at least this fact would be taken care of.

I climbed into the waiting car by myself. The driver put my one suitcase in the trunk and drove away as I looked back at my home, hoping that one of them would leave their room and come out to wish me goodbye and wish me well.

There were no brothers pushing the car, as is symbolic in a lot of Indian cultures, no flowers on the car, and no confetti being sprinkled. I was nervous and scared. I was alone. Walking into a family of strangers, I had no one by my side to hold my hand and tell me it was all going to be all right, that I was just transitioning from one phase of life to another, like normal. Nothing about this felt normal. As much as I wanted out, I didn't want to be so alone. Other than the brother and sister-in-law, his two nieces, and the cousin messenger, I had met no one else in his family.

Halfway down the drive, the car stopped to pick up the cousin. He got into the car and sat next to the driver and told me in Oriya (the language spoken in Orissa), "Don't worry, it will all be fine." It then struck me, I had never spoken Oriya on a daily basis other than conversing with the kitchen help or the rickshaw man who took me places that I needed to go to. In school, Oriya was learned only till the eighth grade, and because I studied in an English medium school as opposed to an Oriya medium school, our instructions and classes were in English. At home we only spoke in English, because that was the common language my grandparents had used to communicate in the early days of their marriage. I was not comfortable having long, drawn-out conversations in Oriya.

As we approached the venue, I saw cars lined up on the side. I saw people walking around all dressed up, and I saw a bunch of women waiting for me with garlands and flowers in their hands. I don't remember if there was music playing. I got out of the car and was immediately surrounded by a group of women who were in their finest saris and had on all the gold jewelry that they owned. At least it felt and looked that way.

I felt ashamed to walk out. With no gold bangles on my wrists, no thick gold chains around my neck, and no dangling pearls or diamonds from my ear lobes, I looked like a poor cousin who had been invited to the party as an afterthought. Only an Indian or someone who understands our culture will understand the significance and importance of this, and how your background, your resources, and your hierarchy in society are judged based on the markers of jewelry and clothes.

Getting out of the car, a lady rushed at me to pull one end of my sari that hung over my shoulder to cover my head. I was asked to walk slowly and demurely with my eyes down towards what seemed to be the center of all the activities. People were teeming all over. I did not know who anyone was. My eyes searched for comfort. A known face. Anyone from my past. Nothing.

As I neared, I saw Arun standing at a distance wearing a silk kurta pajama, a traditional Indian wear for men, waiting for me. Even his clothes seemed more expensive and appropriate than mine. I wondered how people were judging me. He stood next to his mother, who was draped in a white sari, a mark that she was a widow. She also had her head covered. He stood there till I walked up, not touching me or acknowledging my presence in any physical way other than a faint smile. His mother's eyes bore into me, and I could see her assessing my outward worth and standing. I guess I had already failed.

There were chairs around a table. I was asked to sit, and Arun sat in a nearby chair. There was a justice of peace on another chair, and all around us, people were either sitting, standing, watching, or talking. This was the first time in my life that I was amidst so many strangers.

*Desolate and lost on my wedding day.*

As I sat down and looked demurely under my "odhana" veil, which had magically appeared from somewhere on my head, my eyes saw one familiar face in the distance. My uncle's wife. I will always be grateful for that. She, in her own way, with all the restrictions that my grandfather had put around me, had been there for me, nurturing me along the way from a distance. From tutoring me to taking me on local outings, she was there for me in little ways. To date, she is one of the few people who has never forgotten my birthday and is always the first to call me on the day. She was there, but she was there at a distance.

After we signed our names on that document to a few cheers and handshakes, Arun disappeared from my vision. Not wanting to sound eager or desperate, I did not ask anyone about where he was. After lunch was done, I was whisked into a car with his sister-in-law and nieces. On the car ride back, I was told they had rented a home that was large enough to accommodate the people who had come from out of town for the wedding, and that's where we were going.

We arrived about thirty minutes later, and I was told to wait in the car. Some rituals needed to be done before I stepped into their home. A bevy of women came streaming out of the house with thalis (round brass plates) in their hands, making auspicious sounds with their tongue and mouth like many traditional Indians do, especially on the East coast of India. It is supposed to be a sound that waves away evil eyes or evil winds that might blow against you. Not accustomed to this, and hearing my grandfather's words echo that "she grew up very different," this was the first pull of my brain cells coming to life. But I was still enthralled. It felt strange, and yet inclusive. The Indian in me that was not so Christian was liking it.

The women moved towards me, sprinkling rice on my head while I sat in the car. Then they smeared my parting with sindoor, red vermillion powder that in India symbolizes a married woman, and a symbol that in a lot of traditional homes, even today, is never supposed to be washed out or not used. That would mean your husband is dead.

A long veil was thrown over my head and face, and I was taken inside the home, huddled down from my waist. People supported me from all sides like I was old and feeble. I went with the flow. I went with the crowds, each step taking me further away from everything familiar and known. Once inside the home, the inside of which I could not see because my eyes and face were covered, I was taken into a room and plonked down on a four-poster bed. I was propped up against a bolster pillow and had someone settle my sari all around me and was told I could not remove the veil from my head, as people from the neighborhood, mostly women, would be coming to see me. More like check me out and count the amount and number of jewelry pieces I had on.

For four, almost five hours, I sat there while people trooped in. The women held up my face against the light, checking the color of my skin, how dark or light I was, checking to see how fat or thin I was, and asking about who and where my family was. I had already been told not to answer too many questions, and thankfully, sometimes my new sister-in-law or her sister would intervene when people were asking questions and would tell them to leave me alone.

Amidst this zoo and circus, the one person significantly missing was the groom. Finally gearing up some courage, I asked my sister-in-law where he was.

"You won't see him till the eighth. You have to wait four days to consummate your marriage and cannot see him till then. You will have to get married by Hindu rites before that, otherwise his mother will not allow him to come anywhere close to you. This is how Hindu marriages work."

There was nothing I could do or say.

# 20

# *A Second Wedding*

**《 》**

ON THE SECOND DAY, a lot of preparations seemed to be taking place.

"Come, it's your *haldi* ceremony now. We have to get you ready," said my sister-in-law. The haldi ceremony is a purifying ceremony done before a marriage.

"Ready for what?" I asked.

"Your wedding!"

"What do you mean, my wedding?"

"You are having a *bedi* ceremony." (This is a raised platform generally made of brick and mortar with a fire pit in the middle on which most Hindu weddings are performed.) The priest will be here at 1:00 P.M. because the auspicious time is at 1:10 P.M."

"Why a bedi wedding? We were already married yesterday. Why do we need to be married again?" I asked, all bewildered.

"Well, to be accepted as a Hindu *bahu* (daughter in law), you have to be married on a bedi traditionally."

"But how can a Christian marry a Hindu on a bedi?"

"Don't worry, the priest will sprinkle *Ganga* (the Holy River Ganges) *Jal* (water) on you to purify you. And because your name is so Muslim-sounding, they are thinking of changing it to a Hindu name."

At that point, I really did not know what was happening to me or how to deal with it. I was pasted with turmeric, sprinkled with Ganga Jal, and brought to the bedi. Since no one from my family was present, a neighbor was "made" my father in a short little ceremony performed by the priest so that he could perform my *Kanyaa Daan,*

*The Hindu wedding. All huddled up.*

I was devastated, lost, and ignorant, with no say in how my life was being chopped, cut, and pasted to fit so many different dimensions. After the ceremony was over, I was once again relegated to my room for people to view.

On the eighth of August, a wedding reception was hosted by Arun and his family with almost a thousand people there. From my side, my two aunts came, ate, asked me how I was, and left.

In spite of the initial four days of shock, in a lot of ways I looked forward to my new life. How bad could it be? Arun and I were from the same advertising background, I could keep working at the agency, and he was a nice person. He explained to me that he could not say no to his mother when she had asked for all the traditional rituals to be performed.

"She is old, and after my father died when we were young, she raised us with a lot of hardships. How long will she live? Just do a few things to make her happy. Cover your head when you are around her; you don't have to cover it when she is not around. She is a little traditional. Look at my sister-in-law," he said with great pride, "she lives in America, but yet she covers her head when my mother is around."

Yes, I wanted to tell him, if I had to come to India once in five years and cover my head for a month, I would also do it. But I had to live in India, live with eyes on me constantly. I let that fact slide.

And so I embraced my new role in life. We moved to a satellite town a few miles outside Cuttack where he worked at the Textile Mills. The Mill had its own little colony, and the officers were given beautiful bungalows to live in. It was a gated community, and far off from the hustle and bustle of town. The neighbors were mostly colleagues of Arun, and because they were at the same professional levels, they were almost all the same age—so their wives were also the same age, which made them all about two decades older than me. I really had no friends to make that were my age. We had nothing in common: the wives stayed home to cook, sew, or look after their kids. I had given up my job and was home alone all day with no knowledge of how to cook or sew, and no kids to look after.

I would wait till Arun came home in the evenings, and after he caught up with his mother, who lived with us, over a cup of tea, I would ask him to take me on his motorcycle for a ride outside the colony. Because only after I left the gated community could I take off the veil covering my head and feel the breeze and the freedom run through my hair. I don't think I ever told Arun what I was going through. Communication, as you can tell, is not my strongest point.

Arun thought in Oriya and verbalized in English. I thought in English and verbalized in English. Many a thought and feeling were lost in translation between us because of that. Oriya was his first language, and English was mine.

I had not seen my grandparents in months, nor had I spoken to them. I missed them, and yearned for them. I never told anyone, including Arun, about how my heart was breaking for them. Many a time, Arun said, "Let's go see your Papa and Granny. I will win them over. What can they say? The worst they can do is throw me out." For that I will forever be grateful to him.

Four months after I got married, I walked into my grandparent's home on December 24, 1984, which was my grandfather's birthday. It seemed they had aged another hundred years. They were all alone in this huge house, with no one to talk to other than the household help. My heart broke. I felt responsible and guilty, and till this date, I ask for their forgiveness every single day.

Arun was magnificent with them. He treated them with kid gloves and swore to them that he would look after me and told them not to worry about me. It took them a long time to warm up to him, but they did. Never once after that did they tell me I had thrown my life away, or that I would regret anything. They just accepted things the way they were.

In February, I found out that I was pregnant. I craved home and all the food that my grandmother would make. I started to ask to be taken home to my grandparents much more than what was considered normal in a typical, traditional Indian home. Once a girl was married, she was the property of her husband and in-laws. This did not go down well with my mother-in-law.

Her religious beliefs and her being a widow had turned her into a pure vegetarian, with no onions and garlic as part of her diet either. I had had to become a vegetarian at home, and not even garlic was allowed inside the house. I remember eggs and garlic being tied in a piece of cloth and hung outside in the back yard on a tree. I had grown up eating very few vegetables and was basically a carnivore. I lost twenty pounds in the first six months of my marriage.

My mother-in-law was nice in her own way as long as I followed her directions, and there were times she would make me these amazing vegetarian dishes and press my back and feet when they hurt. But she yielded total power over everything else. Her granddaughters, their mother, and almost everyone in her extended family were petrified of her and her sharp tongue. The only two who were not were her two boys. One stayed thousands of miles away and indulged her from afar, and the one she lived with indulged her from near.

The power struggle between us had begun. From trying to limit my social contact with people, to making sure only she had a say in where and how my child was born, little clashes started. I felt I had already changed so much of myself to fit in, to belong, that when I got pregnant, I found a little courage to be who I wanted to be even if it was only with the choices of what I wanted to and needed to eat. As my standing up to her increased a little every day, she would complain to Arun about how insolent I was becoming. He would cajole her, saying I was young, and to be patient with me. With every complaint that she brought to him, the gap between Arun and I expanded.

Things calmed down when my son, Ankoor, was born. He was the first male grandchild. The son and heir. His grandmother doted on him and did a lot for him. However, when she started taking over every aspect of his life, like trying to make him a vegetarian and wanting to name him something that sounded like it came from the Indian Farmer's Almanac, I started to put my foot down. I was responsible for him now. I could not let anyone else make decisions for him.

After a few months, relegated to being at home after my angel was born, I started falling apart. There was no one to talk to, no outlet to vent in, and nowhere to go. My trips to my grandparents had been cut down drastically. I don't know if I suffered from postpartum depression, because that was a word and symptoms I learned of only after I moved to America.

One evening, I started feeling the walls close in on me. I remember being in my bedroom with my baby hardly three months old, and screaming my head off for no apparent or visible reason. Arun and his mother were watching TV in the drawing room. They came running to the bedroom, and after quickly glancing over me, they rushed to shut the windows that opened out to the front yard, lest the neighbors hear.

The Textile Mill doctor was not called in, because that would mean the world knowing. An older colleague couple came instead. Their diagnosis: maybe she is just tired. Give her a sleeping pill and she will be okay by tomorrow. When tomorrow came, and I woke up, everyone in the home went about things like nothing had happened the previous night. That night I think was my first breakdown.

The first time Arun slapped me was when my son was nine months old. He slapped me in the kitchen in front of his mother while the household help was putting away the dishes. I don't remember what exactly was my fault. I might have spoken back to his mother.

I was shocked and I froze. I went to the drawing room, picked up the company phone, and called a childhood friend of mine in Cuttack. I asked him to come pick me up or send a car. He heard me cry over the phone and did not ask or say anything. He just knew. He knew because he was one of the friends who had cautioned me about marrying someone who I had such major lifestyle differences with. Within an hour, the car was there. I had packed a bag for my son and me, and for the first time in my married life, I left the home without Arun's permission. I got into the car and drove straight to my girlfriend's home. Just looking at my face and my disheveled clothes, she knew not to ask anything.

I knew I could not go back to my grandparents, or even tell them what had happened. I had closed that door on myself a long time ago. I could not tell any of my aunts or uncles either, because the only answer or comfort that I would have gotten from them was "I told you so."

Even in that frame of mind, I knew I could not stay with my friend permanently. I had no money to speak off, and neither did she. And my son had started missing his father. I realized it was time to go back. Helpless and hopeless, I returned after a week.

Arun's ego was terribly hurt. He felt that his standing in society had been tainted by all this, even though other than my two friends, no one knew about the little "episode."

We never spoke about it.

I started making more frequent trips into Cuttack, even staying overnight a few times. My grandfather had started feeling unwell, and playing with my son on his lap on sunny winter afternoons on the verandah seemed to be one of the few highlights of his ninety-year-old life.

❲ ❳

On February 18, 1986, my grandfather passed away. I was there, holding his hand and telling him not to be afraid and not to worry about my grandmother. He left seemingly in peace.

The next day the entire city of Cuttack came to a halt. Schools and colleges were closed in respect for his passing, because he was on the board of almost every educational institution. The Baptist church bells tolled from afar slowly and significantly, as they did when someone from the church passed. When his coffin was put on the hearse to be taken to the graveyard, it felt like the entire city was walking behind him. I was proud, so immensely proud.

As the months passed, my childhood friend, who sensed how unhappy I was becoming, became an angel investor and helped me open my own advertising agency. On January 24, 1987, I opened Creators. The first women-owned ad agency in my home state of Orissa. That day, I got a little piece of me back.

I would commute to my grandparent's home in the morning, leave my son with my grandmother, and go to the office. Back around 4 p.m., I would pick up my son and make the thirty-mile trip back to our home in the Textile Mill on the bus that ferried children to the school from the Mill. Things seemed to be looking up for me. I had my son, I saw my grandmother every day, and I had my work. I didn't have to deal with overbearing personalities, or go through any friction on a daily basis. Arun and I barely talked. As was, and still is, my trait, I withdrew into myself when I was wounded or hurt.

In early 1989, Arun's papers to immigrate to America finally came through. I was ecstatic. As much as Arun did not want to go, I wanted to go twenty manifolds more. His brother and wife, for selfish reasons, did not want us to immigrate either. They knew that with our leaving and joining them in America, the burden and onus of caring for their mother was now going to be split between the two sons fifty-fifty. As demure and dutiful as the brother's wife seemed outwardly to be, this was not a load she wanted to carry. Arun was dissuaded many a time from going.

"It is too late for you now."

"You are almost fifty, and you might not find a job here. America is not the same place it was when you were studying here."

"Don't leave your job there. Look at the perks you have there, you will never find that here."

Yes, in hindsight, all this was true. But what they forgot and kept forgetting, even when I got to America, was that I was not even thirty years old, and that I had dreams. I wanted to see the world, live and experience it.

Our marriage had already fallen apart. We barely talked to each other, or even acknowledged each other. Our son was our only common bond. Till today, I don't know how Arun agreed to emigrate. Maybe he thought about his son and that his future would be better off outside of India.

On September 7, 1989, we left Cuttack. I was heartbroken to leave my grandmother. My son was her lifeline, and I had ripped it apart again.

*The day I left my soul behind*
*Was September 7, 1989*
*I left behind a mother dying*
*I left behind friends crying*
*I left behind memories of my life*
*I left behind my soul in strife.*

# 21
# *America*

‹ ›

W E GOT ON THAT TRAIN HEADING TO DELHI,
where our international flight was to leave about
a week later, with six suitcases between us. That
was all that we could pick up from our lives and take with us.
The turnout at the station was tremendous. There was not a
single dry eye. I had already gone home earlier and said goodbye to my grandmother. Leaving her was heart-wrenching.

With the train slowly chugging out of the station and
friends and cousins running alongside the train, the words
out of Arun's mouth were scary and ominous.

"I will never let you leave. I know you think you can go to
America and be happy."

I did not know what to make of it. We hardly talked to
each other anymore. I focused on my son, and he focused on
I don't know what.

As we stood at the baggage carousel in America, waiting for our luggage to arrive, I saw familiar objects roaming free on the carousel. One or more of our suitcases had been damaged in the long haul, and some of our personal effects seemed to have had a mind of their own and were doing the rounds of the carousel. Instead of being embarrassed, I took it as a sign. A sign from the Universe telling me, "If that panty can break free, so can you." Wasn't that the very reason I moved to America? Wasn't this the land where a woman could be a woman, with a voice of her own? With no one to judge, no stigma, I could finally reclaim my life.

Life in America began for me in South Carolina. We were welcomed by his brother and family, but very quickly I began to see the subtle nuances of how we, or really, I, did not belong. My sister-in-law made it a point to constantly talk about the girlfriends that Arun had left behind, the hearts that he had broken, and basically what a ladies man he was. I am not sure to what purpose. One day she went into her garage and pulled out a trunk that had belonged to Arun. In it were love letters, little gifts, and his portrait of the girl he had wanted to marry. I still have the portrait, along with the letters, and many other little mementoes. I laughed it off at that time.

My sister-in-law's life was very clannish. She focused only on her siblings, who were in different parts of the US, and she made sure if they had a family gathering that we were not invited. Arun's brother took a liking to me and would do little things for me. He would take me to the mall sometimes, buy me perfume or clothes, and would try to be welcoming in his own gruff way.

Arun was oblivious of these goings-on. I guess most men don't pick up on little signals under their noses. Eventually fate intervened in the form of Hurricane Hugo on September 22, 1989, which ironically was also Arun's birthday. It brought us to Maryland. The hurricane was a forbearer of tumultuous times to come. After staying for a few months with a cousin, Arun found a job and we moved to an apartment. A couple of months after that, I found a job too, working at Kmart as a sales girl. Not our dream jobs, but definitely a start.

Meanwhile, my soul and mind were getting restless. This was not the life I had envisaged. Arun went to work, came back, and lived for the weekends when he was an active member of a group of people who belonged to Orissa. Each state of India has their own little group in almost every state in the US, and they have one large umbrella organization that meets once a year in different parts of the country. Some of these groups have memberships in the thousands. The Orissa society, I am told, has close to twenty thousand members and is growing, as the H1B Visa status keeps flourishing.

I became a part of that society and was out almost every weekend, either entertaining or being entertained. Since we were new entrants, it was more of being entertained. I had fun at most of the gatherings. My son was growing up with Indian kids on the weekend and not losing sight of his culture and language. Concerts and fashion shows were organized, children were taught about their history, and for the most part, we all came away with a sense of fulfillment.

But like everything in the world, what you see is not what you get. Insecurities, jealousy, competition, and back-biting all seemed to raise their ugly heads. It was all about one-upmanship. Family ugliness came into play. My son would be excluded from a lot of activities that involved his cousins and their cousins. I remember one summer pictures were being taken. My sister-in-law had four nieces and nephews from her side of the family and only one on her husband's side. My son, who was five, did not know the difference between any cousins. He treated them all like his siblings. That day, I remember how his little heart was broken for the first time. A picture was taken of all the cousins and he was left standing out. He cried because he wanted to be in it and didn't understand why he could not. So many things. My sister-in-law came for the summer to her brother's home in Maryland to spend three months babysitting her nephew and niece. Even though I drove past their home every single day to work after dropping my son off at the babysitter, not once did she say, "Drop him off here with me."

With my marriage failing, I had no one to blame but myself. Maybe I was not forthcoming enough with Arun in the beginning. Maybe I made him think I was this demure Indian girl who was traditional in every sense of the word and would toe the line. Maybe he was not who he proclaimed to be, or who the world proclaimed him to be. Maybe that lifestyle that he lived in the US and in India was just a cover-up for being heartbroken. I don't know.

He was a great person as an individual. Great with almost everyone he met. I was not too bad either. Somehow, our stars did not align for us to live in peace and comradeship. Our fights became bitter and acrimonious. He would accuse me of hiding how fractured my life was before I married him. He claimed he had no idea that my parents were divorced, and that if he had known he would never have married me, because no one in his family had ever even thought about the word.

We started hitting out at each other below the belt. I would tell him that as a man he had shirked all responsibilities and was not trying to better himself in terms of a job and a career. I would push to sell his paintings or organize a show, but he would never agree. For all the years that he lived in America, he had the same job at the same level with no ambition to better himself or climb the corporate ladder. Much later, I realized this was his way of punishing me, his way of not letting me go. His words on the train that day make so much more sense now.

I left the marriage so many times. The first time was when my son was seven. I rented a basement room in a stranger's home and shared the bathroom and kitchen with the couple and their three kids. Both my son and I were miserable. He missed his dad, and I could barely make rent. The world did not know what was happening. We still went out for our weekly dinners to friends' homes and to functions. There was not one safe person that I could tell about what was going on, because almost everyone was sitting on the throne of judgment.

After moving out and coming back, realizing and seeing how much my son missed his father and vice versa, I tried to put my despair away. I wanted my son to have both his parents around him; I did not want him to come from a broken home like I did.

I was back at the apartment within a few months. He lived his life and I lived mine, which was basically going to work and back. I had taken a second job and spent large chunks of time outside the home. My son ended up spending so much time with a babysitter, and it was starting to bother me. But I needed things. I needed and wanted a home, a new car, new clothes, summer camps for my son, games and toys for him, unending needs that called for extra income.

Arun did not want any of this. He was content with what he had. He lived his life for the weekends, where he was deeply involved with culture and organizing activities for the community and his weekly hour-long conversations with his brother. My complaints about his family and how they were differentiating between his family and her family fell on deaf ears. In a heated argument one morning: "My brother is my God. Look at how much he has done for us. He brought us here. He educated me. He set up this house for us. I will never go against him or tell him anything. If I was asked to choose, I would choose him over you."

I knew my fate was sealed.

One day, when his family was in town and after a long, bitter fight between us, I reached out to them asking for help. Asking for them to intervene. Asking them for guidance. My sister-in-law said she would come, but an hour later she called to say that she was not coming because she did not know how to help or resolve anything that was going wrong between us. I am sure she came to this decision after meeting with her two-woman counsel of sister and sister-in-law, who seemed to thrive on our home and marriage falling apart.

I realized that day it was sink or swim for me, with my son on my back. Those days, because of my financial resources, it was more sinking than swimming. A couple of years later, I filed for divorce. We both lived under the same roof. He did not respond to my lawyer's notices or messages. He just went about his life and I went about mine. We never talked about it. We still went out together for social events on the weekend. This tells you how dysfunctional the two of us were.

As I found myself swirling towards the whirlpool of depression, one night I told him that I needed help, that I needed to go to therapy. A close friend of mine was in therapy and had told me how she benefitted from it.

"We Indians don't need therapy. What will my family think? Therapy is expensive and we don't have the money for it."

"You could apply for another job, or get a second job?"

"I am old now, I cannot work two jobs." He was sixty and I was forty.

# 22

# *A Healing and an Illness*

❨ ❩

AS THE DYSFUNCTION IN OUR MARRIAGE CONTINUED, I was still haunted by my rejection at the age of fourteen by the person I wanted to marry, the eyes of classmates who looked away when they saw my face, and the eyes of the people who I passed on the street who would never look at me twice.

In 1999, armed with a health insurance package that was amazingly encompassing, I flew to Dallas, Texas, for my third surgery. After a complicated and long surgery, I was wheeled out with one rib missing, a very small price to pay for a nose that disappeared when I was fourteen. At thirty-eight, I finally felt pretty again. I could finally throw away my hideous glasses and show my face to the world. I could finally let a picture be taken with a side profile. The wait and the journey were long and expensive in more ways than one, but it restored my confidence, or at least some of my confidence.

Finally doing a little better financially, and with my son in high school, I moved out once again. I rented a home nearby so that my son could stay close to his school and father. I continued to pay the mortgage for our home and the rental for where I lived. If I did not, the house would have gone into foreclosure. That was something I could not let happen. That was the home my son grew up in. I could not do that to him.

What I did not realize was that I was doing worse to him. All my back and forth was not helping him at all. My beautiful, gregarious boy grew up to be a quiet introvert. After two years of living at the rental home, I dropped my son off to college. Three months after that, I got laid off from my work.

With no money and just unemployment to get by, I could not afford the rental. Back I went again to the only base camp I knew. And so we lived under the same roof in different rooms like we had done for the last twenty years of our life. A year later, I found a job that could once again sustain me and I left.

I was almost forty-six. Life was half over. Yet I soldiered on with no promise of a future that would bring peace, happiness, or direction. My family in India and his family in the US had no idea that we were separated. When they came to visit, I would come back to the house, clean and cook for them, and pretend I lived there. Thankfully, they did not stay the night, and once they left, I would leave too.

One summer, a cousin and his family came from India to visit for a week. Since they did not know we were separated, I moved back into the house and went about life like no disruptions were in place. Together we went to places as far away as New York. Arun was with us, and the six of us had a good time. This side of him, when he was with people, was how he shone. He loved that interaction. But when it came back to the two of us, we both failed miserably.

Though we did not live together, Arun and I still kept in touch. We still had our son, who was in college, and the shared mortgage to bind us. He refused to sell the house, and said he would leave only when he was dead. He did not care that paying the mortgage was becoming a struggle. To help with the costs, I took the initiative and gave a room out to rent. As much as he hated the idea and opposed it, I stood firm.

In July of 2009, on his way back from the annual Oriya convention in New Jersey, Arun called me at work to tell me he had taken the next day off and was going to ask our son to drive him to Johns Hopkins in Baltimore. His brother, who was also a doctor, had recommended he go see this particular doctor since he was constantly complaining of back pain.

Never wishing anything bad for him, I told him to keep me posted.

On July 10 of 2009, the day his PET Scan report was due, I went with him to the oncologist. The doctor pulled up the scan and showed us how, other than his brain, his whole body was covered in red. He had stage 4 cancer. The doctor asked me to walk outside with him, and told me that Arun had a maximum of six months to live. There was no hope, no cure, but as a doctor, he wanted to give chemo a try just in case something worked.

I drove Arun home after the doctor's appointment. I could see how defeated and lost he felt. The cancer had spread so quickly that within days, he was homebound with no energy to go to work or outside. One more time, I packed up my apartment and moved back home to take care of him.

By mid-July, he was too feeble to be left alone at home. I took leave from work and stayed home twenty-four seven. He had chemo sessions a couple of times, but each time seemed to make him worse than the previous. After talking to his doctor, the family and I realized chemo was not helping.

He was hospitalized twice. After they stabilized him, they realized he needed morphine to manage the immense pain he was in, and he was moved to a nursing facility. The morphine helped in little ways. I would sit with him when he was awake, and he would look at me with tears running down his eyes. "Thank you," one day he mumbled. "Don't leave me here alone to die. I want to go home and die."

The days my son came to see him, his face would light up with joy. My son would just sit with his dad, holding his hand for a long time.

When the morphine stopped helping, he had to be moved to hospice. I wished to God I did not have to do that. Thankfully, his brother decided to make that decision for all of us. Arun was moved to Hospice on the 14 of August, 2009. I stayed the night there, making sure he was comfortable. On the morning of the fifteenth, I went home for a quick shower after telling him that I would be back in an hour. He was not cognizant, but I still felt the need to tell him that so that he did not feel abandoned. Twenty minutes down the road, the hospice nurse called me: "Your husband is gone."

I pulled over to the side of the road and bawled my eyes out. Grief that a human being was gone. Sadness that I was never able to be someone he wanted. Guilt that he was alone when he left the world. What if he had opened his eyes and not seen a known face? He had asked me not to leave him alone, and that is what I did.

And most of all, I was aware of his words to me on the train: "I will never let you leave."

He finally left on his terms, and his life.

August 15 is celebrated as India's Independence Day. It felt like he, with his immense love for India, had chosen that day for his own independence. Independence from the pain he was in, and independence from a marriage that he was not cut out for.

But he never let me leave. For twenty-five years and eleven days, he never let me leave.

# PART IV

(( ))

PART IV

# 23

# *The Past Comes to the Present*

**S**OMETIME IN 2015, MY CELL PHONE RANG.
I looked at the name that flashed on my phone's screen: a name that I knew, someone who hardly ever called me. The name that flashed had first called me when my grandmother had passed away.

I picked up my cell and the uneasy churning in the pit of my stomach started. The man at the other end of the line was my mother's husband. I have never addressed him as anything, not Dad (he is not my biological father), not Uncle, not even by his first name.

Her husband called to tell me that he didn't think she would live long.

I listened, asked a few questions, "What happened? Does she have a full-time nurse? Is she on medication? Is she eating?,"and hung up the phone.

What I really wanted to ask was,

"Why did she abandon me?"

"Has she never asked about me?"

"Did she ever love me?"

On the fifth of October, 2016, I left for India. I flew into Mumbai and took a flight to the town I was born in, the town where I grew up, got married, and had a child. A town that both shunned me and loved me for the twenty-three years that I lived there. It is a complicated relationship that I have with my town.

A fortnight before I was to leave for India, a friend and I were sitting on my deck in the suburbs of Maryland, watching the sun set and sipping wine. I go back to India once a year in October to host a writer's retreat in a part of the country that is far, far away from the town that I was born. We talked about the retreat, the participants who had registered that year, and the different programs we were offering.

"How is your book coming along?" my friend asked, knowing that I was in the midst of working on my memoir.

"It's going." That was my usual answer to everyone who asked that question. What I really wanted to say, and could not say, was "I don't know how to end it."

Deep down in my heart I knew that was not really true. All I had to do was ask questions and find my answers and my book would wrap itself up. But how does one who has never felt entitled to their history and life even begin that process? Somewhere, my childhood was locked away, and I didn't seem to have the courage to confront myself, to harness my memories and put them on paper in black and white.

"I am going back to the place where my story began to see how it ends." As soon as I said these words to my friend, I knew that I was finally ready. I don't know if it was the sunset, the wine, or the sheer exhaustion of living in the shadows.

I also knew that the person I needed answers from was my mother. She had suffered a stroke a couple of years earlier and was slipping into dementia. The days she was alert, she did not ask questions. The days she was not alert, the only two questions she had were about the two "other" children. She was afraid they had been kidnapped. She wanted to know if they had been found. Her husband tried to tell her that both her kids were there, but she kept saying she had two more.

She had a few lucid moments, but they were few and far between, I was told. She was failing to recognize people, even the ones who were close to her, and was relapsing into the past. I knew my time to get my answers was running out.

I knew it would be a tough journey. Having been raised in a household where there were no heart-to heart talks, where family name and what we projected to the world was far more important than how we were feeling, I didn't even know how to begin.

As I sat in that plane for the two-and-a-half hours it took me to get from Mumbai in the western part of India to Cuttack in the eastern part of India, my stomach was churning and knotting. Here I was, going into a household and a past where I had no place or no home. I was not sure how to maneuver my physical being, my mental state, and my emotional state. Would I be shunned, would I be looked upon suspiciously, or would I be just someone who was trying to create trouble by stirring up pots of the past?

*What is my purpose?* This question kept gnawing at my insides. Some friends and some of my cousins didn't quite know or understand why I wanted to thrust myself into a clock or a time warp that I could never turn back.

Driving from the airport through the crowded streets of my little town to get to where my mother lived, I passed through streets and alleys that were at once familiar and alien. I saw a little girl a long, long time ago who wandered the streets hoping to catch a glimpse of the life she could have lived. Searching but still not connecting. She was not shy, but ashamed to exist.

There was no turning back now. I was there. A quick prayer from my lips to give me strength, to keep me poised, and most importantly, to not hurt my half-siblings in any possible way.

On the seventh of October, I walked into the room my mother was confined to. I was warned before I went in that she was mixing up people, was not getting names straight. She was living in the past as a young girl with her parents and her siblings.

My sister-in-law held my mother's hand while I stood in front of her. She asked, "Mummy, do you know who this is?"

My mother looked up, a faint smile playing on her lips. Her eyes were fading and greyed. She held my right hand. "What do you mean? Of course. That is my daughter, Shabnam. we call her Bubu at home. Why do you think I will not recognize my own daughter?"

There was so much indignation in her voice. For a moment, I forgot that this was the first time that she had publicly acknowledged me as her daughter. The first time I was someone's daughter. The first time I was my mother's daughter.

I was fifty-five years old that day.

# 24

# Questions

《 》

She looked at me with those eyes
Those brown eyes
Those eyes that I saw every day
In the mirror when I brushed my teeth
In the mirror when I combed my hair
Did those eyes recognize my face?
Did those eyes see her own eyes
reflected in my eyes?
Did she see the question in my eyes?
And did she have the answer in her eyes?
Dementia, do I see you reflected in her eyes
or is the reflection a shadow of regret
that she hides behind?

STAYED IN HER HOME FOR TWO NIGHTS AND THREE
DAYS, the home where she lived with her husband, with
my half brother and his family and her in-laws all spread
along the compound. This was a home that for years I had
wanted to come see what was inside. To see how she lived.

The three days that I was there, not once did she forget my name. Every few hours, she would ask if I had eaten. Every few hours, she would ask if I had slept. But she would never forget my name. Her eyes would follow me each time I walked across the room, stood up to get a glass of water, or just sat.

I was garnering up my courage to ask her the questions that have always weighed heavily on my mind. I needed to be alone with her for a few minutes. I needed to have that one-on-one interaction with her. But in the three days that I was there, she was never left alone. Her husband was always close. Always aware. I think he realized or knew I was there to get answers.

The night before I was leaving, seeing there was no chance of my talking to her alone, I decided to ask the next best person. The person who in my mind was the one who had enabled her to walk out of the house. The person who had seen a child and had still pulled the mother away.

"Why did she leave me?"

"Do you really want to know, now?" my mother's husband asked. "Let it be, what is to be gained? She is living her karma now. I never knew this would be her fate and my fate. I am bearing this burden now."

"Yes, I need to know. Did she ever miss us?"

"Your father was very cruel to her. She had to leave him and come away. He used to hit her. I wanted to adopt you, but your grandfather said no."

As soon as he said that, I knew I was not getting the truth. I would never get the truth from him.

What he did not know, and still does not know, is my grandfather's legacy to me. The copious notes left behind in two bound books. The diary.

I left the conversation alone and went back to my room to pack. My half brother sat on my bed, looking defeated. It was the first time he and I had met after he found out that I was his sister. As a father himself, he could not understand why his parents had done what they did. I felt defeated myself, and wondered if I would ever know the truth.

I left the next morning. I walked into her room to tell her I was leaving. I saw tears in her eyes. She held my hand gently.

"You are leaving? Will you come back?"

"Yes," I said, "I am leaving." Leaving because this is not my home. Leaving because you left me fifty years ago. Leaving because there was never any place by your side or in your heart for me. This is what I wanted to say, but never did.

I walked into the waiting car and looked back at the home that housed her. I had the heavy feeling in my heart that this was it; I would never see her again.

I never got the answers that I was looking for, but my mother's eyes told me a lot. In this lifetime that I am living, I have to accept that this will be the most that I will ever know. I know it might not be today, but it will be a tomorrow when I will get a call to say that she is no longer here. There are so many questions and no answers. I know I will never know the truth, but even that is okay. I have found my place in this world, I have found my feet, and most importantly, I have found myself.

*March, 2017*

After I came back from seeing my mother, I began to understand maybe why she did what she did. When she met her second husband and decided to marry him, this seemed to be the only lifeline she was getting for a second chance in life. Being a divorcee in the '60s in a small town was not looked upon favorably. To make sure her life and future were secure, she chose love for her self over love for her children.

The person she chose to marry came from an Orthodox Hindu family. When he met her, he was still doing his undergraduate degree. He was young and lived at home with his parents. She was older than him, was a working woman, was of a different faith and had two children from a previous marriage. Not marriage material at all.

Falling head over heels in love with her, he chose to present her to the world as someone who was not encumbered with anything or anyone. He was ashamed of her past. She was not good enough to be presented to his world as she was. She was given a choice of him or her children. She chose him. To appease the world and strangers, she gave up on the only two people that she could really call her own.

I hear that my mother has been highly agitated for the past few months. She keeps asking about these two children she had, the ones she could not see anymore. She was afraid for their safety and was concerned that they were being abused. She is also unable to recognize her husband. She asks the people around her, who is this strange man? She wonders why he is in her room.

# *Epilogue*

## *Fall Seven Times and Stand Up Eight*

### —JAPANESE PROVERB

❨ ❩

THE PERFECT MOTHER I HAVE NEVER BEEN. My son has seen hard and dark times, but again, love and only love has kept us going. I never gave up on myself, and I never gave up on him. When I told him I was writing a book and there might be some hard facts about his father, who he loved, and that I was a little worried about what my family or my half-siblings might feel, he said, "Painters paint, writers write. You write your story, don't worry about what anyone will say or think." I am blessed to be his mother.

There have been countless evenings where I sat on my bed with the lights off, the room dark, or got into my car to drive around aimlessly while all the water in my body fell through my eyes. But however dark, misty, foggy, or rainy my view was, I always had hope. I always had hope that there was something better for me waiting to happen. It propelled me forward. Hope did not let me die.

I have love in my life. Hope and resilience? Never give up on them. They will find their way into your life if you keep the door of faith open. Believe in yourself even when the world around you is filled with disbelievers.

I might not have the energy to do the things that I wanted to do decades ago, but I have realized that is okay. In my sixth decade, I can finally smile and be spontaneous. I can be who I am without being judged for being a girl, or for being someone who did not fit in, or for just being. Where there is hope, there is hurt, and to love deeply is to risk hurting deeply. But where there is Light there will always be love.

And one day soon, I will write a story about love. About falling in love when you are not looking for love.

At the end of our lives it is how we are loved that defines our life.

# Acknowledgements

( )

T O MY GRANDPARENTS, who have given me all that I
have known, all that I have seen, and all that I have
done. You picked me up and rescued me from a life
that is unknown. Because of you both, I have some sort of
history and some roots. I wish I could go back and tell you
how much I loved you both, and how much I now understand about what you did. I am sorry for the hurt, and I am
sorry for the pain I caused. When I think of the word "parents," a picture of the two of you is in my mind and no one
else. Papa, thank you for your writings; without those diaries,
I would not know who I was and am.

To Arun, I hope you understand my need to write this
book. I wrote about the truth; I wrote about our life. You and
I were distant planets orbiting this space called life, and we
were never aligned.

To my half siblings, Godhuli and Goutam, thank you for your understanding. Thank you for standing by my side. I know reading this will be difficult for both of you, but I wrote about the woman who was my mother, and not the woman who is your mother. Keep the thoughts of your mother in your minds and cherish those memories. I was just a by line.

To Abhijat, my husband, who I have to thank for giving me the space to write this book and the ability to create the Panchgani Writers' Retreat. If it was not for the retreat, I do not think I could have completed this book. Thank you for the support.

Thank you to Sanjeewan Vidyalaya and Shashitai, chairperson of Sanjeewan Vidyalaya Trust, and the principals and the staff, who for the last four years have been instrumental in the success of the Panchgani Writers' Retreat.

To Allison McCarthy, my first ever editor, thank you for doing such a fabulous job in getting me to publish in *Brain, Child* magazine—my first publication! It's the little edits that count. Peggy Moran, my editor from WWCR, thank you for being the first to shape my book.

To Dede Cummings, my publisher, Rose Alexandre-Leach, my editor, and Katri Nykanen, the visiting intern, all from Green Writers Press. This book would not exist without you.

To Steve Eisner, from When Words Count Retreat, thank you for recognizing the flickering light of a writer in me.

To Steve Rohr, thank you for that late night conversation in Vermont and encouraging me to never give up.

To Filomena Thompson, my amazing cover designer, what can I say? Don't judge a book by its cover is a common phrase, but in this case so untrue. Judge a book by its cover, is what is being said!! Thank you!!

To my Rasho Family in Turlock, CA, especially my uncle, Daniel Rasho. I am so blessed to have connected with you all after almost four decades. I am sure my grandmother, Susember, and your dad, Nicco, are in heaven together celebrating. I know some of the places and languages mentioned in my book might not be accurate, but I could only go on what my memory of my grandmother's stories were. Maybe we will write a book together.

To my precious boy, Ankoor, you are where I begin and end.

There are so many people in my life who I have not named, but have come to mean so much to me along this journey. I will always love you for the Light you bring to my world.